VAUGHN J. FEATHERSTONE

As the Father Hath Loved Us

LEATHERWOOD
PRESS

Leatherwood Press books are available exclusively
through Deseret Book Distributors.

For details write or telephone
Deseret Book Distributors, 40 East South Temple
Salt Lake City, Utah 84111, (801) 534-1515

Leatherwood Press LLC
8160 South Highland Drive
Sandy, Utah 84093
www.leatherwoodpress.com

Table of Contents

Appreciation

My wife, Merlene, has been a supreme and wonderful example to me and to our children. She has motivated me greatly in all that I have done. She is an elect and regal woman.

I thank our daughter, Jill, and our six sons, Ronald, David, Joseph, Scott, Lawrence and Paul. They have all been faithful and prayed to a loving and kind Heavenly Father after our accident, and we believe God heard their prayers.

Thanks to Annette Brunson who typed the manuscript. She has many talents and wonderful skills. She has served as secretary to the Logan Temple Presidency for eighteen years. She is loved by all who know her.

And thanks also to Leatherwood Press, particularly Timothy Robinson and Britney Schetselaar who edited and prepared the manuscript for publishing.

A special thanks to our son, Scott, who wrote the book "Hallelujah" about the life of George Frederick Handel and the coming forth of the "Messiah." He gave strong encouragement for me to write this book.

And God bless the apostles and prophets—the pinnacle example of Christ-like behavior. I love and sustain them with all my heart.

Forward

For some significant period I have felt to write some strong and tender feelings about the Father of us all. It is most fitting that we talk so much about the Savior—His loving kindness, His nobility, His Godhood, His relationship to God, the Eternal Father and His magnificence. We read His works constantly. We pour over the scriptures. We emulate His teachings. We revere His holy name. We comfort each other with His words. He is the exemplar, the model, the only true and living Christ. He is in our thoughts and our actions. His teachings cling to those of us who love and worship Him.

There is so much recorded about His life, His ministry, His divinity and His work and service. We are want to exclaim, *Oh, the grandness, the goodness, the charity and mercy of our Redeemer.* In our deepest sorrows and most profound trials we seek the peace that comes only through Him, that peace that "passeth all understanding" (Philip. 4:7).

In our follies like Alma, we plead, "Oh, Jesus, thou Son of God, have mercy on me, who am in the gall of bitterness" (Alma 36:18). By and by, when we have been through the repentance process, we feel that profound sense of relief that comes to those who accept Him as the Redeemer of the world.

So much more could be said about the Savior. And the purpose of this work is not to undo any of the feelings, attitudes, loyalties, testimonies or supreme faith and love we have in Him. Instead, it is to focus for a time on the majesty of God, the Eternal Father.

My personal focus and steadfastness have centered in our Lord, Jesus Christ, and His life, redemption, atonement and teachings. Somehow, in spite of the fact that we pray to our Father in Heaven, our intense teaching, love and interest have gravitated toward the Savior and all His doings. I have spoken more about Him in my ministry than anyone or anything else in the world.

By contrast, I have spoken much less about God, the Eternal Father. My love and intense desire to please Him has been constant. He simply, through my preoccupation, has not been as constantly prominent in my thoughts as He should always be. Even in my prayers, my heart seems to center on the Master and His unconditional love.

For some years now I have had a change of heart and have come to a realization of the Father's majesty, His wonderfulness, His glory, His unfathomable concern for each one of us. Think of the greatness and the goodness of our loving Father in Heaven. Now, I pray differently. I focus on Him in a magnified way. I have always loved and reverenced Him and have sought to do His will and please Him; but my main focus has been on His Only Begotten Son.

Now I understand a lot more about this supreme being that begot each one of us, literally, as our spiritual Father. The hope of this book is not to de-emphasize in the smallest way the feelings and tenderness we have for the "Incomparable Christ," but to bring additional focus and realization that God, the Eternal Father is the author and designer of "the great plan of happiness," to provide a redeemer, to provide an atonement to satisfy the demands of justice and to extend mercy to His children. The great plan of salvation is God the Eternal Father's program for His children. The Savior accepted the program and volunteered to do all that our Father would command Him to do. We need to focus on the Savior and God the Father with a reverence, love and gratitude unmatched in the eternities.

In some small way, I would like this book to be the means of an increased awareness of all that God our Father has done and is doing without diminishing in the smallest way the ministry of our Lord and Savior.

Our Father in Heaven

"Our Father which art in heaven, Hallowed be thy name. Thy kingdom come. Thy will be done in earth, as it is in heaven" (Luke 6:9–10).

When we pray, we are instructed to pray to our Father in Heaven. It is He who hears and answers our prayers. It is He who puts all things and His servants in motion to grant us the pleadings of our heart. In this most fundamental way, our relationship with the Father underlies all that we know spiritually.

During a recent accident involving my wife and me, several things happened that were significant to us. We had just attended a meeting just outside Afton, Wyoming. The night was clear, not a whisper of wind. An officer of the law had stopped us, told us one of our tail lights was out and reminded us to watch for deer and elk along the highway.

The speed limit was 65 miles an hour. I put the car in cruise control at 65 and watched way down the highway for the eyes of elk and deer.

Two horses were galloping toward us at about 20 miles an hour on the side of the road. I never did see them, as they were off the left corner of the car. We hit them and I was knocked unconscious. My wife was miraculously unharmed, but I suffered some critical injuries. I was taken to the medical center in Afton. Then I was life-flighted to the LDS Hospital in Salt Lake City. The surgeons reconstructed my face and sewed me up while my family gathered outside in a waiting room.

The accident took place on Wednesday night. The next night the family stayed till a late hour. I regained consciousness at about midnight or 1:00 a.m. When I awoke, the room was dark. I could not see. I called out, "Is there anyone here?" My son Joseph responded, "I'm here, Dad." I faded off again until several hours just before dawn. When I awoke the second time I called out, "Joseph, are you still here?" From somewhere in the dark room came the response, "I'm still here, Dad."

Joseph was there all the next night as well. My other son Scott was on a high council and had to attend a stake dance. After the dance he came and sat with me too. Our sons and daughter were all there throughout the day. I would hear them as I faded in and out. It was a great comfort to me.

In a way, this singular experience is not unlike that of millions of our Heavenly Father's children who call out to Him in their hour of need. One of the great acts of goodness of our Father in Heaven is that when we are in desperate trouble, when we think we are all alone, we cry out in our agony, "Are you there?" and that sweet feeling of peace and assurance comes to us in our mind, "Yes, I am here."

Sometimes conditions in life drive us to our knees, humble us to the dust of the earth, try our souls beyond what we feel we can stand. In those agonizing moments, all pride, arrogance, achievements, successes, etc., are stripped from our souls. We come to a point where we know that no power on earth can rescue us; we require divine help and intervention. The very act of prayer itself, the humbling and becoming meek, can begin the healing process for we know that He, the God and Father of us all, hears and answers every prayer. He can surely hear and respond to ours.

It is not difficult to understand the power of God to answer the prayers of every soul on the earth when we know of the experience Moses had when he "beheld the earth, yea, even all of it; and there was not a particle of it which he did not behold, discerning it by the spirit of God. And he beheld also the inhabitants thereof, and there was not a soul which he beheld not; and he discerned them by the Spirit of God; and their numbers were great, even numberless as the sand upon the sea shore" (Moses 1:27–28). And Enoch "beheld all the families of the earth" (Moses 7:45), and in another place the scriptures say "and it came to pass that the Lord showed unto Enoch all the inhabitants of the earth" (Moses 7:21). The brother of Jared also saw "all the inhabitants of the earth which had been, and also all that would be; and he [God] withheld them not from his sight, even unto the ends of the earth" (Ether 3:25).

How is it possible to discern the particles of the earth or all the inhabitants from the beginning unto the "ends of the earth?" It was accomplished through their spiritual eyes, not their natural eyes, and through the Spirit of God.

The great and beloved Father in Heaven can discern all this and more. What limits would man, in his ignorance, dare to put on Him? If Moses, Enoch and the brother of Jared could behold the particles of the earth "and there was not a particle of it which he did not behold" (Moses 1:27); and if they beheld the inhabitants of the earth, all of them with their spiritual eyes, and this they did in a moment in time, then what powers does God the Father of all have? Indeed can He not with His limitless power, in His omniscience and omnipresence behold each one of His children individually?

We ought to keep upmost and most prominent that God in heaven loveth His children. We need to subject ourselves to Him. He is our great and grand king of heaven and earth. We ought to ever be mindful of our relationship to Him as

His spiritual children—to know He is always there watching over us and to treasure up his words.

The prophet Alma helps us to understand the blessings of nurturing in our souls the good word of God.

> *But if ye will nourish the word, yea, nourish the tree as it beginneth to grow, by your faith with great diligence, and with patience, looking forward to the fruit thereof, it shall take root; and behold it shall be a tree springing up unto everlasting life.*
>
> *And because of your diligence and your faith and your patience with the word in nourishing it, that it may take root in you, behold, by and by ye shall pluck the fruit thereof, which is most precious, which is sweet above all that is sweet, and which is white above all that is white, yea, and pure above all that is pure; and ye shall feast upon this fruit even until ye are filled, that ye hunger not, neither shall ye thirst.*
>
> *Then, my brethren, ye shall reap the rewards of your faith, and your diligence, and patience, and long-suffering, waiting for the tree to bring forth fruit unto you. (Alma 32:41–43)*

It is God our Father, through the instrumentality of His Only Begotten Son, Jesus Christ, who has provided us with the iron rod, the tree of life, and the gospel, which are all part of His great plan of happiness for us. There comes trailing down from the preexistence, in the deep recesses of our soul, a dependence upon our loving Father. In our moments of agony, terror, death, and overwhelming burdens our inner soul cries out to Him. Somehow we feel that He and only He can bring peace to our overburdened souls. He never fails to answer in His perfect way and with His perfect love and with our eternal welfare as His focus.

Amulek taught that we should "exercise...faith unto repentance, that ye begin to call upon his holy name, that he would have mercy upon you" (Alma 34:17). He continues:

> *Yea, cry unto him for mercy; for he is mighty to save.*
>
> *Yea, humble yourselves, and continue in prayer unto him.*
>
> *Cry unto him when ye are in your fields, yea, over all your flocks.*
>
> *Cry unto him in your houses, yea, over all your household, both morning, mid-day, and evening.*
>
> *Yea, cry unto him against the power of your enemies.*
>
> *Yea, cry unto him against the devil, who is an enemy to all righteous.*
>
> *Cry unto him over the crops of your fields, that ye may prosper in them.*
>
> *Cry over the flocks of your fields, that they may increase.*
>
> *But this is not all; ye must pour out your souls in your closets, and your secret places, and in your wilderness.*
>
> *Yea, and when you do not cry unto the Lord, let your hearts be full, drawn out in prayer unto him continually*

for your welfare, and also for the welfare of those who are around you. (Alma 34:18–27)

Our prayers will be heard and out of the depths of our suffering there will come sweet and tender whisperings that we are not alone; that somewhere in the realms of Heaven, He knows, He understands and He will bring us peace and healing.

Our prayers to Him should focus on our Father, the great Elohim, and we should acknowledge before His throne our absolute and total willingness to accept whatever befalls us, knowing that our eventual becoming like Him is through our submission and obedience to Him.

All around us are choice examples of just such submission. The late Elder Neal A. Maxwell of the Quorum of the Twelve Apostles is a marvelous example of a totally dedicated disciple who bore all. He suffered through knowing that God could have delivered Him in an instant. We learn much when we suffer for righteousness sake. You can imagine a loving Father who has cradled and held close to His bosom a beloved, oh so faithful disciple and apostle, Elder Maxwell. Alma declared that "the spirits of all men, whether they be good or evil, are taken home to that God who gave them life" (Alma 40:11). My, oh my, what a tender, incomprehensible experience for our beloved and dear friends, Elder Maxwell and Elder David B. Haight, when their Father and our Father, their God and our God, embraced them and welcomed them back home to their just rewards. Truly the scriptures are fulfilled that state "no tongue can speak, neither can there be written by any man, neither can the hearts of men conceive so great and marvelous things" (3 Nephi 17:17) as a loving Father would feel and share with a beloved son or daughter returned home.

When we pray, let us remember we are praying to our Father in Heaven and let our minds and hearts focus in love, gratitude and sweet tenderness on Him as His children.

The Eternal God

*I*n his Sermon on the Mount, the Lord teaches us how to address God in prayer: "Our Father which art in heaven, Hallowed be thy name. Thy kingdom come. Thy will be done" (Matthew 6:9). He is the Eternal God and it is His Kingdom that will come.

Further, in teaching us how to pray, the Lord directs us to say, "and lead us not into temptation" (Matthew 6:13).

The poet Harry Kemp reminds us of how close we often come to yielding to temptation in his poem "Prayer." He also reminds us from whence the power of deliverance comes.

A Prayer
by Harry Kemp

I kneel not now to pray that Thou
*   Make white one single sin,*

I only kneel to thank Thee, Lord,
  For what I have not been—
For deeds which sprouted in my heart
  But ne'er to bloom were brought
The monstrous vices which I slew
  In the shambles of my thought.
So for the man I might have been
  My heart must cease to mourn—
'Twere best to praise the living Lord
  For monsters never born,
To bend the spiritual knee
  (Knowing myself within)
And thank the kind benignant God
  For what I have not been.

Sometimes we look back through our lives and see that some unseen hand directed us away from sin and sorrow. Temptation is part of life. As President McKay has reminded us, no act is ever committed without having first been justified in the mind. This is what Harry Kemp is expressing in the above verse. We battle the temptations in our minds and there we choose to submit or resist.

But in this battle we are not alone. Each of us has been given the light of Christ. It lighteth every man and woman. The light of Christ beckons us to choose the right. It is something like a homing device. It points the way homeward to our Eternal Father.

Over the years my wife has heard me speak about homing pigeons. During the time I presided over the Texas San Antonio Mission we attended a sacrament meeting in our home ward. A member of the Bishopric was the speaker. He stood up, lifted a large paper grocery sack that was on the stand and put it on the pulpit with his books. The paper sack moved enough that everyone knew there was something alive in it. He had the rapt attention of the children and youth. Part of the way through his talk he opened the sack and withdrew a homing pigeon. He held the pigeon where everyone could see and taught us that a homing pigeon has a brain about the size of a pea. He said in that pea-sized brain there is a "homing device" that guides the pigeon safely back home. He said, "we live 12 miles from here and before I finish speaking this pigeon will be back on its perch at our home." He left the stand went down to the side door of the chapel, stepped outside and let the pigeon loose. The speaker returned to the stand and drew parallel after parallel.

I have long been fascinated by homing pigeons. When a pigeon is turned loose it lifts into the air and begins to circle wider and wider and higher and higher. Then, in some incomprehensible way, it determines the right direction to fly homeward and is gone. It is an amazing thing to see.

Archie Brugger, the temple president at the Manti Utah Temple, used to raise homing pigeons. He said he would put them in the back of a his van and drive 400 to 450 miles away. He would stop the truck and let the pigeons out. He said they would lift into the air, circle wider and wider, and higher and higher, and then this special God-given gift to homing pigeons would kick in and lead them in the right direction back to home.

Dr. James O. Mason, a former General Authority and Head of the Communicable Disease Center in Atlanta, Georgia, also used to raise homing pigeons. He once told me how he would take them to a distant city, Los Angeles, for example, and turn them loose. He had a sophisticated timer that would print out the precise time on a band which he would then secure around the pigeon's leg. Then he would drive back home and await the pigeon's arrival. He said they would feed the pigeons on a diet of peas, corn and beans and the pigeon's pectoral muscles would swell to an inch thick. He informed me that homing pigeons seldom took time to stop to eat. They typically only stop for water. The timed homing pigeons made the trip from Los Angeles to Salt Lake in about 13 hours. When they arrived home their pectoral muscles would be worn down to about one eighth of an inch thick.

One homing pigeon was sold by a man in Long Island, New York, to a man in Guatemala City, Guatemala. Somehow the pigeon got out of the coop and flew across the Gulf of Mexico, across the southern part of the United States, and eventually back to its former roost in Long Island. There are even accounts of homing pigeons flying from as far north as Anchorage, Alaska, back to the Northwest.

Recently my wife received an assignment to speak at a stake Primary fireside in Logan. In preparing for her talk, she called a boy named Jonathan Francis in nearby Smithfield. Jonathan was in an accident years ago and has overcome some serious physical problems relating to his injuries. He is a wonderful, thoughtful, sensitive young man and he raises homing pigeons. Merlene asked if she could use one of his pigeons to demonstrate the principle of homing patterns. Jonathan and his mother dropped off a large metal bird cage with the pigeon. The pigeon was taken from its roost put in the back of their van at night and dropped off and put inside the shed at our residence. Merlene transferred the bird to a paper sack, taped the top closed and took the bird to the Primary fireside. The pigeon could not see to orient itself. The next evening she shared information about homing pigeons.

The question my wife raised with the Primary children was, "If God would put a homing instinct in a pigeon, wouldn't he do it for His children here on the earth? We all have an internal homing device and the signal is clear and unmistakable. As we listen to the Spirit we are guided safely away from pitfalls, temptations, counterfeits, diversions, perversions and evil."

The prayer by the Master "and lead us not into temptation" is what our Father in Heaven intends to do for us if we ask and hallow His holy name. The light of Christ lighteth every soul. Our conscience is a constant reminder if we heed the warnings and do not become calloused in our daily conduct. For those who have received it, the gift of the Holy Ghost acts to guide us and warn of dangers.

In the morning and at night, we pray to the Being who is the pinnacle of all knowledge, power and wisdom, the perfect being, God our Eternal Father. We pray in the name of His Only Begotten Son, Jesus Christ. When we truly pray "with real intent" and with great "faith in Christ" (Moroni 10:4), God will bless us and, with our special homing device, lead us back to Him, a glorious and beloved Father.

He is the eternal God, the perfect judge, the architect of the plan of redemption and salvation, the physical Father of His Only Begotten Son, the controller and governor of the heavens and the earth. He is the power by which worlds without number have been created. There is no beginning nor end to His kingdoms. He is the one true and living God and to worship Him brings eternal rewards. We become joint heirs with Christ in all that our Father hath (D&C 84:37–38). He has perfected His knowledge, wisdom and there is nothing in which He is not perfect. He is supreme and His love is unconditional. He has provided the program and designed the course that will lead us back home to His presence. Man with his puny mind cannot comprehend the smallest particle of His majesty.

Under "God" in the Topical Guide there are numerous references. It is a humbling experience and a grand privilege to read the many references. I will refer to a few—"Eternal Nature of God," "Gifts of God," "Glory of God," "Indignation of God," "Intelligence of God," "Justice of God," "Love of God," "Mercy of God," "Perfection of God," "Power of God," "Presence of God," "God the Father—Elohim," etc.

Is it any wonder that the obedient, the humble, the meek, the poor in spirit, the truth seekers, the peacemakers, the pure in heart, the God-fearing, the honest, the faithful, the virtuous, the suffering, all seem to find in Him that peace that surpasses understanding and the strength to endure any trial that may come? Oh, how we ought to love and worship Him. Oh, how we ought to express our gratitude and thanksgiving and oh how we ought to secure His love and will in all we do and say. This is a time to ponder on the majesty of God and make some special commitments as to our total submission to His divine will for the rest of our lives.

You may want to take 15 minutes with a pen and paper and write down your deepest, most impressionable feelings about our Father in Heaven. This will be a treasured witness and testimony for generations who follow you to know the feelings of your heart and soul for God.

When Through the Deep Waters

In July 1972, President Joseph Fielding Smith passed away. President Harold B. Lee was set apart as prophet, seer and revelator of the Church. The first Thursday of August 1972, the general authorities met in our normal first Thursday temple meeting in the upper room of the temple. It was a solemn occasion. President Lee had been set apart but a solemn assembly would not be held until October Conference to sustain him.

President Lee conducted the first Thursday temple meeting. He suggested that for our opening hymn we should sing all seven verses of "How Firm a Foundation." I recall thinking "President Lee, I want to hear you and the brethren speak. All seven verses would infringe on that time." I love the hymn but selfishly I wanted the time for the prophet's remarks.

I knew the first three verses so I did not have to look at the hymnal. As we sang the fourth and fifth verses I looked up to the front of the room at the prophet. He was looking above us in the air, the tears were coursing down his cheeks. To see this great soul weep caused me to shed tears of my own. I could hardly read the sixth and seventh verses. I don't know what he saw or whether he saw anything. I dared not look.

You will recall that President Lee lost his wife not too long before being called as President of the Church, then he lost a daughter as well. I have long thought and pondered over the last four verses of "How Firm A Foundation." How very special they are. After that meeting I committed all seven verses to memory. Over the years I have quoted it when the occasion seemed appropriate. Each time I do, I can see that beloved and holy man in my mind's eye weeping as he sang:

> *When through the deep waters I call thee to go,*
> *The rivers of sorrow shall not thee o'erflow,*
> *For I will be with thee, thy troubles to bless,*
> *And sanctify to thee thy deepest distress.*
>
> *When through fiery trials thy pathway shall lie,*
> *My grace, all sufficient, shall be thy supply.*
> *The flame shall not hurt thee; I only design*
> *Thy dross to consume and thy gold to refine.*

E'en down to old age, all my people shall prove
My sov'reign, eternal, unchangeable love;
And then, when gray hair shall their temples adorn,
Like lambs shall they still in my bosom be borne.

The soul that on Jesus hath leaned for repose
I will not, I cannot, desert to his foes;
That soul, though all hell should endeavor to shake,
I'll never, no never, no never forsake!

— *"How Firm a Foundation," Verses 4–7*

This has become one of my favorite hymns. I can only imagine what President Lee was thinking as all the body of General Authorities sang "when through the deep waters I call thee to go, the rivers of sorrow shall not thee o'er flow." I could only imagine that he felt the closeness of his first wife and daughter. I would also suspect of all the places in eternity the Savior might have been, it would be near his beloved servant Harold B. Lee during this trying time of his life. In some small way we can understand that our Father in Heaven watched that temple scene with 10,000 times more compassion and God-like softness and love and understood the white heat crucible through which President Lee had been asked to go.

I have to admit that I have long felt a particular closeness to President Harold B. Lee. When I was 17 or 18 I ruptured a disc in my back. I was in great pain and it looked as though I might need a costly operation to restore my strength. About that time, President Lee came to speak at our stake conference. I listened to this great, strong, powerful leader talk about the Master and illuminate gospel principles. I was spiritually saturated with a witness of how great this man was.

At the end of the meeting I stood in a line to shake hands with President Lee and when it was my turn I said, filled with faith, "Elder Lee, would you give me a blessing?" This great man looked kindly and humbly at me, an older teenager from a broken home, clothed not quite as well as others but in the best I had; he said softly, "Son, why don't you ask your Bishop? He has the priesthood and can give you a special blessing." I wasn't disappointed. I just accepted his counsel, thanked him and left.

The next week I went to my Bishop and asked him for a blessing. I'm certain President Lee just didn't let my request drop. He must have pointed me out to the Stake President who was from our ward. He probably wanted to make sure I received a proper blessing. The Stake President, Harry T. Oscarson, knew the conditions in our home and I am sure he knew which family I was from. He had been our Bishop earlier.

When I approached the Bishop, he seemed to know what had happened when I asked Elder Lee for a blessing and what counsel I had received. Our Bishop was Wilford W. Kimball, a great and holy man. He was kind. He was prepared. He gave me a wonderful blessing and I was content.

Like the great God of Heaven, President Harold B. Lee worked through the appropriate leaders to respond to a member's need. I have never had a need to have surgery on my back. It was a miracle at the hands of my good Bishop.

Since the first time I heard President Lee speak and felt close to him, I used him as a personal pattern for living. I wanted to do everything and be everything that I knew he would want us as Church members to do and be. He must have been my priesthood leader in the spirit world. He always seemed to me the perfect example of a pure warrior with an unbreakable will to do what God would have him do. That is what makes what happened later in my life so tender.

When I was called into the Presiding Bishopric on April 6, 1972, it was President Lee who called our home in Boise. I was out in the field riding with our three-year-old daughter Jill on the "boys" Honda 70.

I received word from a neighbor boy that President Harold B. Lee was waiting for me on the phone. President Lee was a counselor at the time to President Joseph Fielding Smith. I hurried home as quickly as I could and answered the call. President Lee was on the phone.

He said, "President Featherstone (I was Stake President), we are asking you to make the most momentous decision of your life."

My response was, "What is it President Lee?" It wouldn't have mattered what it was. I would have said yes to anything.

He said, "President Joseph Fielding Smith and President Nathan Eldon Tanner are here on the speaker phone with me." After a few comments he announced, "The Presiding Bishopric are being released at this conference. The Lord has called Victor L. Brown to serve as the Presiding Bishop and the Lord has called you to serve as 2nd Counselor in the Presiding Bishopric." He gave me instructions and told me I could tell my wife but no one else until after it was announced at General Conference.

The day we were ordained Bishops and set apart at the Presiding Bishopric was the Sunday after Conference. President Joseph Fielding Smith presided over the meeting, President Lee conducted.

With the most tender feelings in my heart, I remember offering a silent prayer to God our Father. "Heavenly Father, if it's not asking too much, can I please have President Lee ordain and set me apart?" There were five men to be set apart—three from the Presiding Bishopric and Bishop John H. Vandenburg and Bishop Robert L. Simpson who had been called as assistants to the Twelve Apostles.

When it was my turn, President Harold B. Lee said, "I think I would like to be voice," to which President Joseph Fielding Smith agreed. I received a marvelous blessing from President Lee.

I was certain he could not have remembered the request for a blessing which I had made of him twenty-three years earlier. I believe, however, that God our Eternal Father remembered. This time my request and prayer of my heart was an appropriate one; and our Father in Heaven permitted me to receive a long-desired blessing from his special servant, Harold B. Lee.

In our wonderings and with our limitations, we must forever stand in awe at the myriads of conditions which our God in Heaven never forgets. He responds where it meets His divine will for us and in his own ever-mindful ways.

I have also been fortunate enough to be on the receiving end of such tender, merciful promptings. Many times. Once, a few short years ago, I was visiting the Kaysville Crestwood Stake. President Bott was the Stake President. During the general session of conference on Sunday I said, "President Bott, I think your choir is wonderful. They can sing anything. Would you ask them to sing 'Be Still, My Soul.'" President Bott said, "When?" I said, "Now. This is a good time."

The choir began to sing. I looked at President Bott and he had tears in his eyes and on his cheeks. I said, "Tell me about it." While the choir sang on he said, "Thirty years ago I served a mission in Germany. I served for 30 months and did not baptize one soul into the Church. Early on m y mission I heard 'Be Still, My Soul.' I memorized it and sang it when I was lonely or rejected. It was a great blessing throughout my mission. Thanks for having the choir sing it."

I remember thinking, "I love God." I imagined the message He was sending to President Bott: *I was there. I knew it was tough. I knew you didn't baptize anyone, but I didn't forget. You are here. You are the Stake President. I have been with you all through those 30 years as well as on your mission.* I had not asked a choir to sing that hymn before—I believe it was inspiration.

Who is this God who can hear the tiniest whisper of a prayer or the agonizing cries of those who turn to Him.

We are taught patience and we are taught that "His will" will be done. There are so many prayers answered by that God who gave us life that we may only be aware of a few. When we know all things we will know "face to face," for "then shall I know even as also I am known" (1 Corinthians 13:12). We will know the supreme goodness of God the Father, Elohim, and His watchful care over us all the days we lived and through the eternities.

The Majesty of God the Eternal Father

In the first chapter of Moses we read these stirring words:

> The words of God, which he spake unto Moses at a time when Moses was caught up into an exceedingly high mountain,

> And he saw God face to face, and he talked with him, and the glory of God was upon Moses; therefore Moses could endure his presence,

> And God spake unto Moses, saying: Behold, I am the Lord God Almighty, and Endless is my name; for I am without beginning of days or end of years; and is not this endless?

> And, behold, thou art my son; wherefore look, and I will show thee the workmanship of mine hands; but not all, for my works are without end, and also my words, for they never cease.

> *Wherefore, no man can behold all my works, except he behold all my glory; and no man can behold all my glory, and afterwards remain in the flesh on the earth.*
>
> *And I have a work for thee, Moses, my son; and thou art in the similitude of mine Only Begotten; and mine Only Begotten is and shall be the Savior, for he is full of grace and truth; but there is no God beside me, and all things are present with me, for I know them all. (Moses 1:1–6)*

We assume that Jehovah is speaking quoting our Father in Heaven in the same way we quote exact words of prophets and the Savior.

Moses has the privilege of beholding the "workmanship of [His] hands" (1:4). Moses beheld many lands and their inhabitants as he stood in the presence of God (Jehovah) (1:27, 29). Jehovah continues quoting the Father.

> *And by the word of my power, have I created them, which is mine Only Begotten Son, who is full of grace and truth.*
>
> *And worlds without number have I created; and I also created them for mine own purpose; and by the Son I created them, which is mine Only Begotten. (Moses 1:32–33)*

All these things we ascribe unto God. He has created worlds without number. Then, He, God the Father, being quoted by the Savior states:

> *And the Lord God spake unto Moses, saying: The heavens,*

they are many, and they cannot be numbered unto man; but they are numbered unto me, for they are mine.

And as one earth shall pass away, and the heavens thereof even so shall another come; and there is no end to my works, neither to my words. (Moses 1:37– 38)

We have many varying opinions regarding astronomy. They may be as accurate as man can comprehend with our limitations. It has been stated that the Milky Way Galaxy is 600 billion miles across and that there are 400 to 600 billion stars in it. There are other lesser estimates and projections which are beyond calculations. The Hubble telescope circumnavigates the earth about 300 miles out. A recent article in *National Geographic* revealed that if you point the Hubble telescope into the least populated area of the cosmos at something the size of a grain of sand held on the end of your finger and your outstretched arm that there are layer upon layer of galaxies. Then you have to ponder 360° in every direction at the more heavily populated cosmos and the article concludes that there may be millions or billions of galaxies.

We are here and we are going somewhere. In His goodness the Lord declared, "This is my work and my glory—to bring to pass the immortality and eternal life of man" (Moses 1:39).

It was the Father who directed Jehovah and Michael to

form, beautify, bring life and create all the wonders about us. In a simplistic comparison it is the architect who designs a wonderful structure and the builder then builds according to the plan. The earth was part of God's eternal plan for us and the Savior became the creator.

God our Father is the Supreme Being in the eternities. He designed the plan of salvation and provided His children with moral agency. Agency is an eternal, God-given principle which provides choice or volition to accept or reject this program for us. The eternal principles, commandments and doctrines were designed for us as part of this plan of salvation.

In the 19th section of the Doctrine and Covenants, the Lord clarifies and simplifies our understanding of agency. Through revelation, the Savior shares His feelings about the atonement and the trial it was to Him. He described it in these words with a commandment.

> *Therefore, I command you to repent—repent, lest I smite you by the rod of my mouth, and by my wrath, and by my anger, and your sufferings be sore—how sore you know not, how exquisite you know not, yea, how hard to bear you know not.*
>
> *For behold, I, God, have suffered these things for all, that they might not suffer if they would repent;*
>
> *But if they would not repent they must suffer even as I;*
>
> *Which suffering caused myself, even God, the greatest of all, to tremble because of pain, and to bleed at every pore, and*

to suffer both body and spirit—and would that I might not drink the bitter cup, and shrink—

Nevertheless, glory be to the Father, and I partook and finished my preparations unto the children of men. (D&C 19:15–19)

In verse 17, the Lord implies that there are only two choices in life—to suffer or to repent. There isn't a third option, no fourth, fifth or tenth choice. We repent or we suffer. Those of us in the Church have chosen to repent and accept Christ as the Redeemer of the world, the Savior, The Atoner, and the Only Begotten of the Father who is full of grace and truth. The Savior is perfect. His ways are just and true and are the course necessary to lead back to eternal life with our Father.

In God's great plan, we are given commandments—tithing, the Word of Wisdom, repentance and baptism, faithfulness, priesthood for the brethren, temple marriage, and all the others. To each is affixed a promise. God is good and gracious. He commands us to pay tithing and when we do, He opens up the windows of heaven and pours out blessings we cannot contain (see Malachi 3:10). We live the Word of Wisdom and He promises that we "shall run and not be weary, and shall walk and not faint. And I, the Lord, give unto them a promise, that the destroying angel shall pass by them, as the children of Israel" (D&C 89:19–21). We will have health in the navel and marrow in the bones (89:18).

We have to understand the majesty of God when we consider that it is He to whom our Savior appeals as our advocate. In the 45th section, the Lord declares that we should...

> *Listen to Him who is the advocate with the Father, who is pleading your cause before Him—*
>
> *Saying: Father, behold the sufferings and death of him who did no sin, in whom thou wast well pleased; behold the blood of thy Son which was shed, the blood of him whom thou gavest that thyself might be glorified. (D&C 45:3—4)*

And then these humble, sweet words, "Wherefore, Father, spare these my brethren that believe on my name, that they may come unto me and have everlasting life" (D&C 45:5).

Of all the beings who ever have or ever will walk the earth, we have for an advocate the one perfect being, the literal physical Son of God. But He to whom the Savior is pleading—He who will ultimately grant the unparalleled blessing of everlasting life—is our beloved Father in Heaven.

We are taught by the Savior in 3rd Nephi how to pray. In verse 9 of chapter 19 it states, "and they did pray for that which they most desired; and they desired that the Holy Ghost should be given unto them." The reason we pray for the Holy Ghost when we pray is that He will inspire us as to the things for which we should pray.

The Holy Ghost will never err in the things he inspires us to say and do. He is also perfect and abides with us as we prove worthy. There are resplendent blessings that come to us as we pray as guided by the Holy Ghost. These are the prayers that appeal to God in His loving kindness and goodness.

For the most part we should be guided by the Holy Ghost in our prayers. Then we will seldom pray for issues or things, guidance or direction, that are not pleasing to God.

Enos was taught in a marvelous way. He bears testimony stating:

> *Behold, it came to pass that I, Enos, knowing my father that he was a just man—for he taught me in his language, and also in the nurture and admonition of the Lord—and blessed be the name of my God for it—*
>
> *And I will tell you of the wrestle which I had before God, before I received remission of my sins.*
>
> *Behold, I went to hunt beasts in the forests; and the words which I had often heard my father speak concerning eternal life, and the joy of the saints, sunk deep into my heart.*
>
> *And my soul hungered; and I kneeled down before my Maker, and I cried unto him in mighty prayer and supplication for mine own soul; and all the day long did I cry unto him; yea, and when the night came I did still raise my voice high that it reached the heavens.*
>
> *And there came a voice unto me, saying: Enos, thy sins are forgiven thee, and thou shalt be blessed.*

> *And I, Enos, knew that God could not lie; wherefore, my guilt was swept away.*
>
> *And I said: Lord, how is it done?*
>
> *And he said unto me: Because of thy faith in Christ, whom thou hast never before heard nor seen. And many years pass away before he shall manifest himself in the flesh; wherefore, go to, thy faith that made thee whole. (Enos 1:1–8)*

After Enos has been told that his sins are forgiven due to the faith he has in the Lord Jesus Christ whom he had "never before heard nor seen" (verse 8), then his heart is turned with a "desire for the welfare of my brethren,…wherefore, I did pour out my whole soul unto God for them." Then he declared, "the voice of the Lord came into my mind again" (verse 10). The Lord comforted Enoch after he "prayed unto him with many long strugglings for my brethren, the Lamanites" (verse 11). These are comforting words in verse 12: "I will grant unto thee according to thy desires, because of thy faith." Enos shares what his prayer had caused him to desire—how he was led to pray for that which was right. Lehi, Nephi, Jacob and other prophets before him had likewise prayed that the records of their people might be preserved (verse 13). He was told that "thy fathers have also required of me this thing; and it shall be done unto them according to their faith; for their faith was like unto thine" (verse 18). Like these great prophets, we too can be taught that for which we should pray if we will listen to the promptings of the Spirit.

Oh, the goodness and the majesty of the plan of our Father. He has provided every blessing and opportunity to return to His presence with beloved mothers, fathers, husbands, wives and children. His prophets, inspired by the Holy Ghost, have recorded those things that are essential for us to do to be exalted with eternal lives. And we can receive our own guidance directly from the Father as we make our way back to His presence.

When we pray, let us focus on the Father of our spirits, let our "hearts be full, drawn out in prayer" (Alma 34:27). These are the prayers He answers through His loving kindness. And this is available to every soul that has walked, walks, or will walk the earth.

Perhaps, if we fully understood His powers, His glories, His total knowledge, His greatness and grandness, His creations, His realms, kingdoms and principalities, we might be fearful of kneeling in His presence. But in His goodness, He has invited all to come before Him and pray. And "if it be right," their prayers are granted. The most humble sinner or transgressor can know that as they "finally" come unto Him, He is there and will bring peace and hope even in their wayward condition.

Pray, oh pray unto our God our Father with all the power of your souls and He will always be there.

The Marvelous Works of God

As we consider God, the great architect of the plan of happiness, the plan of salvation and the eternal rewards, we consider Christ the builder, creator of His work.

Moroni declares:

> For do we not read that God is the same yesterday, to-day, and forever, and in him there is no variableness neither shadow of changing?
>
> And now, if ye have imagined up unto yourselves a god who doth vary, and in whom there is shadow of changing, then have ye imagined up unto yourselves a god who is not a God of miracles.
>
> But behold, I will show unto you a God of miracles, even the God of Abraham, and the God of Isaac, and the God of Jacob; and it is that same God who created the heavens and the earth, and all things that in them are.

> *Behold, he created Adam, and by Adam came the fall of man. And because of the fall of man came Jesus Christ, even the Father and the Son; and because of Jesus Christ came the redemption of man.*
>
> *And because of the redemption of man, which came by Jesus Christ, they are brought back into the presence of the Lord; yea, this is wherein all men are redeemed, because the death of Christ bringeth to pass the resurrection, which bringeth to pass a redemption from an endless sleep, from which sleep all men shall be awakened by the power of God when the trump shall sound; and they shall come forth, both small and great, and all shall stand before his bar, being redeemed and loosed from this eternal band of death, which death is a temporal death....*
>
> *Behold, are not the things that God hath wrought marvelous in our eyes? Yea, and who can comprehend the marvelous works of God. (Mormon 9:9–13, 16)*

Of course this passage refers to Christ, but the Son is like unto the Father. All that He is and does is in obedience to His Father's program. They are inseparable in cause, will and stature. All that Mormon suggests about the Lord Jesus Christ in the above verses reflects the Father's will and His divine plan, the creation, Adam, peopling the earth and the glorious gospel and the celestial teachings.

"Yea, and who can comprehend the marvelous works of God?" (Mormon 9:16). The prophet Joseph Smith's ministry is one of the marvelous works of God.

Of all the souls who will walk the earth in our sphere of time, Joseph, a young man of faith, intellect and yet relatively unschooled was selected by the greatest being in time and eternities to perform a monumental work of restoration. His ministry was one of such consequence that we must marvel at the circumstances of the First Vision. This young man in his fifteenth year, having read James 1:5, grasped the full import of that verse and, having faith, sought the God of Heaven for answers to his concerns about finding the true Church. Following the scriptural pattern, he found a secluded place of reverence, quiet and beauty. Early on a spring morning he did what he had been taught to do—ask of God in faith.

Unquestionably his prayer would have begun in the usual way: "Father in Heaven," or "Beloved Father," or "Dear God," or some such phrase. And yet the answer to that simple prayer, the personal visitation by the very personage to whom he had addressed his prayer, placed him among the very few throughout history who have been privileged to behold Elohim.

The Father had put the restoration of His Church and His priesthood into motion. It was His will that Joseph be called to the work. "One of them spake unto me, calling me by name and said, pointing to the other—*This is My Beloved Son. Hear Him!*"" (Joseph Smith—History 1:17). How hallowed to hear the voice of God the Eternal Father.

Other prophets in history have had visions of the Father. Lehi was overcome by the Spirit. He was carried away in a vision "and he thought he saw God sitting upon his throne, surrounded with numberless concourses of angels in the attitude of singing and praising their God" (1 Nephi 1:8). A little over five centuries later, Alma the Younger, going through the process of repentance, declares that "methought I saw...God sitting upon his throne,...and my soul did long to be there" (Alma 36:22).

At the time Jesus was baptized, the Father declared out of the Heavens, "This is my beloved Son, in whom I am well pleased" (Matthew 3:17). Peter bore witness:

> *For we have not followed cunningly devised fables, when we made known unto you the power and coming of our Lord Jesus Christ, but were eyewitnesses of his majesty.*
>
> *For he received from God the Father honor and glory, when there came such a voice to him from the excellent glory, This is my beloved Son, in whom I am well pleased.*
>
> *And this voice which came from heaven we heard, when we were with him in the holy mount. (2 Peter 1:16–18)*

Again in 3rd Nephi the record states, "Behold my Beloved Son, in whom I am well pleased, in whom I have glorified my name—hear ye him" (3 Nephi 11:7). There were 2,500 souls who were witnesses that the voice of God spoke to them on that blessed day.

And yet, Joseph actually heard his name spoken by that eternal God of Heaven. We can only stand in awe and wonder at the majesty and rapture beyond expression of having the Father call you by name. And yet we are all spirit children of that same God and He knows our names as well.

Our conversation through prayer to that God, who designed an eternal plan for our own personal welfare and who provides a way whereby we can be like unto Him, should be very personal. We reverence Him in our daily prayers by kneeling with bowed head and closed eyes before uttering the ponderings of our hearts.

In a recent conference talk, President Hinckley felt to include a prayer as part of his talk. Those of us who witnessed this remarkable event will not soon forget his appeal to God in our behalf and the tender feelings he expressed toward our Father. It was a sacred and special few moments when the heavens seem to part and we could feel the love of our prophet for his and our Eternal Father.

There is no dark corner of the earth, no recess so black, no closet so hidden, no jungle so deep, no forest so thick, no place on this broad expansive earth from which the simplest prayer of a humble believer could not be heard ... and answered.

Our faith in our Father, our awareness and understanding of Him, His mighty work and His love for all of His children should draw us to Him.

God's Love, "The Pure Love of Christ"

The 19th section of the Doctrine and Covenants gives us some understanding of God's love. The Savior declares His identity in verse 1.

"I am Alpha and Omega, Christ the Lord; yea, even I am he, the beginning and the end, the Redeemer of the world."

He is the Redeemer of the world and in verse 3 He shares His greatness. He states, "retaining all power, even to the destroying of Satan and his works at the end of the world." Then He reminds us of "the last great day judgment, which I shall pass upon the inhabitants thereof, judging every man according to his works and the deeds which he has done."

In all eternity God the Father has never given so much power and authority to another living soul. Surely His confidence in His Only Begotten Son is absolute. The Christ teaches that every man must repent or suffer. These are the only two choices we have an opportunity to make with our moral agency while in this life:

> *And I would that all men might be saved. But we read that in the great and last day there are some who shall be cast out, yea, who shall be cast off from the presence of the Lord;*
>
> *Yea, who shall be consigned to a state of endless misery, fulfilling the words which say: They that have done good shall have everlasting life; and they that have done evil shall have everlasting damnation. And thus it is. Amen. (Helaman 12:25–26)*

The suffering will include woes, weeping, wailing and gnashing of teeth for those who are thus tormented with eternal damnation.

> *Wherefore, he saves all except them—they shall go away into everlasting punishment, which is endless punishment, which is eternal punishment, to reign with the devil and his angels in eternity, where their worm dieth not, and the fire is not quenched, which is their torment— (D&C 76:44)*

The atonement, for those who repent, is one of the most gracious gifts of the Redeemer. As we consider the magnificence, the charity, the love, and the glories that await us in eternity, we should be profoundly grateful, even humbled to the dust of the earth as Moses was. Every time we think or consider the atonement we ought to be driven to our knees in the purest expression of gratitude to our Father and His Only Begotten.

Listen to the Savior's testimony and witness as to the depth and suffering and affliction through which He passed:

> *Wherefore, I command you to repent, and keep the commandments which you have received by the hand of my servant Joseph Smith, Jun., in my name;*
>
> *And it is by my almighty power that you have received them;*
>
> *Therefore, I command you to repent—repent, lest I smite you by the rod of my mouth, and by my wrath, and by my anger, and your sufferings be sore—how sore you know not, how exquisite you know not, yea, how hard to bear you know not.*
>
> *For behold, I, God, have suffered these things for all, that they might not suffer if they would repent;*
>
> *But if they would not repent they must suffer even as I;*
>
> *Which suffering caused myself, even God, the greatest of all, to tremble because of pain, and to bleed at every pore, and to suffer both body and spirit—and would that I might not drink the bitter cup, and shrink— (D&C 19:13–18)*

He ends with this wonderful tribute to the Father: "Nevertheless, glory be to the Father, and I partook and finished my preparations unto the children of men" (D&C 19:19).

The atonement was unquestionably the greatest test for the Savior of the world. Remember His own witness:

"and would that I might not drink the bitter cup, and shrink" (19:18).

Our Eternal Father knew the exquisite pain and suffering causing His Son to bleed at every pore. We know the suffering was all inclusive, not only the collective justice required to satisfy its demands for all the sins, transgressions of the repentant; but also for all the pains and afflictions, sicknesses, infirmities and trials of the righteous as well.

In my book *The Incomparable Christ* I have a full chapter entitled "Justice According to the Supreme Goodness of God." In that volume I suggested that it would not be just if only the sinner or transgressor could have their suffering atoned for. More often than not the innocent who suffer, the quadriplegic, incest victim, cancer victim, divorced, etc., suffer far, far more than the guilty sinner. It said,

> *When we really believe that Christ will take upon Himself our afflictions, our illnesses and sicknesses, we will do what Alma and King Lamoni's father did. We will go to Him who can take the weight of our trials and sufferings from us. The Master in his loving goodness will surely bring relief to the innocent victims of horrible deeds as to those who transgress. That is true justice.* (The Incomparable Christ *11*)

The innocent deserve an atonement for their innocent suffering and that is just. He knows how to succor His children in their trials. The purpose of this chapter is to remind us lest we forget that as difficult, exquisite and hard to bear as was the atonement for the Savior, it may have been far more difficult for the Father. Even in our weakness, most of us find that we would gladly trade places with our children rather than watch them pass through exquisite suffering. The one being in all eternity who understands the depths of suffering physically, mentally, emotionally, spiritually to the greatest depths through which the Savior suffered, is God the eternal Father. When the experience in Gethsemane was over we, in our infant spiritual understanding, can only imagine that Elohim wept from empathy and love for His Only Begotten who "suffered all" and declares "nevertheless, glory be to the Father, I partook and finished my preparations..." Yes, the Father suffered the pain and anguish with His Son as we do with our children.

The statement to the Father: "Behold the blood of thy Son which was shed, the blood of him whom *thou gavest* that thyself might be glorified" (D&C 45:4). "For God so loved the world that he gave his only begotten son" (John 3:16).

We can only imagine the love of a divine parent who willingly allowed the suffering of His beloved son in Gethsemane as well as on Golgotha's Hill when he could have intervened with a word. We cannot fully grasp the magnitude of the gift we have been given—the blood and life of His "Only Begotten" for the world.

This single act ought to saturate our minds, hearts and souls with the divine love of a supreme God for all His children. The one perfectly obedient, submissive soul among all the children of men was required to pay the price to satisfy the demands of justice.

We must not forget the Father's role in this pivotal part of the great plan of happiness. It was the Father's will that the price be paid so that His wayward children could be rescued for the eternities.

We must also wonder if the plan requiring a Savior who would suffer nigh unto death was part of the plan which Lucifer could not accept. By forcing all of God's spiritual offspring to live the commandments there would be no need for a Savior. Every soul would have been forced to be perfectly obedient. Could Satan have known that, He could never have gone through voluntarily, of his own volition, what our Redeemer went through. He never would have nor ever could have been absolutely and totally obedient, willing to suffer in such an exquisite way and give all the honor and glory forever to our Father in Heaven.

In our hearts and souls we must let our gratitude and love for God ascend up forever and forever.

Imagine the Father amidst worlds without number, plans for redemption, the work of the atonement, and His eternal ministry, which we know so little about. And yet in all His majesty, He hears the tiniest whisper of a prayer from the least of all His creations and cares and responds with an answer. We must wonder at His eternal doings as one eternity rolls upon another and worlds without number pass away. Who is this Father of our spirits who declared through His prophet Moroni: "Has the day of miracles ceased? Or have angels ceased to appear unto the children of men? Or has he withheld the power of the Holy Ghost from them? Or will he, so long as time shall last, or the earth shall stand, or there shall be one man upon the face thereof to be saved?" (Moroni 7:35−36).

Our Father in Heaven, hallowed be thy holy name.

Thy God Shall Be My God

In the Book of Ruth, we read that Elimelech and Naomi had two sons, Mahlon and Chilion. During a famine, the family journeyed to the land of Moab where Elimelech soon died. Naomi's sons found wives, Orpah and Ruth. They dwelled together in Moab for close to ten years. Then Mahlon and Chilion both died.

In her sorrow, Naomi was about to journey back to the land of Judah when she turned to her two daughters-in-law and said, "Go, return each to her mother's house" (Ruth 1:8). She appreciated that the two women had dealt kindly with her two sons and with her. Orpah kissed her mother-in-law and went back unto her people.

But Ruth clave unto Naomi and made an appeal that has rung down through the centuries. It is a sweet, generous call to husbands and wives and has been such through the generations since Naomi and Ruth: "And Ruth said, Intreat me not to leave thee, or to return from following after thee: for whither thou goest, I will go; and where thou lodgest, I will lodge: thy people shall be my people, and thy God my God" (Ruth 1:16).

Couples who are having serious marital problems would be wise to quote this over to themselves. Any two people can get along and resolve problems and concerns if they will practice Christian principles. Those who have fallen out of love can fall in love again. They did it once, they can do it again. Over the years I have counseled couples in the hope of holding marriages together. Any marriage can succeed if the husband and wife have a commitment to each other—*thy God will be my God.*

Another powerful tool for strengthening marriages is the temple. The House of the Lord is among the greatest blessings that our Father in Heaven has vouchsafed for us in this life. There is perhaps no other place where we can find such direct access to the powers of heaven. Our faith is strengthened, our families are strengthened, and we are strengthened as we attend the temple.

A young couple with three or four children was in the process of getting a divorce. They loved every one else and couldn't stand each other. The Bishop had counseled them to the point where he felt he had little else to say to them.

They were both worthy and held temple recommends. They just couldn't stand each other.

Finally in desperation, the Bishop said, "Will you do one last thing?" The couple said, "We don't want the divorce, we love our children, we love the Lord; but we don't think God would expect us to be this unhappy for the rest of our lives."

The Bishop, desperate, said, "Will you go to the temple next Friday night and then sit in the Celestial room and talk softly to each other for 20 or 30 minutes, then do that for the next four weeks, then return and tell me what happened." The couple went to the temple Friday night and sat in the Celestial room and talked. An interesting thing—you can't yell in the Celestial room. You can't argue. The couple sat and talked in subdued voices. They returned to the temple the following Friday night and through the month.

At the end of the experience the husband returned to the Bishop and said with emotion, "Bishop, thanks for not giving up on us. We talked in the temple. I talked and my wife listened, she talked and I listened. I fell back in love with my wife and she has fallen back in love with me. Our children will not be without one or the other of their parents. I have come to love my wife more than I ever had before. Thanks for saving our marriage."

Our Father in Heaven has provided temples where we might do a holy and sacred work for our kindred dead. We find peace, love and inspiration when we go to the temple.

The God of Heaven, in His grand design, proclaimed temples would provide the necessary ordinances and covenants that would open the door to exaltation and eternal lives.

Many people searching for answers go to the temple. They meditate, ponder and pray. These prayers ascend to the Heavenly Father of us all. When we go through the trials of death as Naomi did losing her husband and both sons, we seem to be utterly helpless and we drop to our knees or slip over to the temple and turn to a kind, sweet loving Father who wants us to feel comfort and healing as any mortal mother or father would.

Recently I was in the baptistry at the Logan Temple. I observed a baptizer baptizing a man of about 30 years of age. The baptizer would baptize him then wait almost a full minute before baptizing him again. We had ten or so young men and women waiting in the little baptistry chapel. I went in and greeted the youth and their leaders before walking back to the font area. The baptizer was still baptizing this brother and taking about a minute between each ordinance.

At an appropriate moment, I stepped forward and quietly said to the baptizer, "Is there a reason you are going so slow?" One of the witnesses replied, "We are having an experience." I could not see the face of the man being baptized so I walked around to the other side. He was crying. I thanked them and left the baptismal area. Then I went to another part of the temple and sat with the patrons who were waiting to do an endowment. All of a sudden I realized what had been happening.

I went back to the font area. The baptizer was still there, but the person being baptized had left. I said to the man who was baptizing, "Thank you for being sensitive even though I was insensitive. Tell me what happened." He told me that the man had done research and prepared cards for his immediate ancestors and relatives who had passed away. He would be baptized for one and as he would come up out of the water, he would weep and shudder with emotion for the person for whom he was proxy. They would have to wait until he had control of his emotions then they would baptize him for another deceased member of his family. Each one was so personal and the man being baptized was so overcome with emotion that a flood of tears would come. It happened with every single baptism until he had finished his family's work.

Imagine the blessing God has provided through His temple that vicarious work can be done for our progenitors. If they accept the work done for them, they will receive every blessing those of us who have been active all of our lives will receive. The God of Heaven has this marvelous perfect plan that provides an opportunity for every soul who ever lived, who lives now, or who ever will walk the earth to receive exaltation and eternal lives.

Later that same day, I was in the baptistry again. I watched a man baptize a woman who was about his same age. After the baptism the man and woman stood there in the font and embraced. Tears were flowing freely down the man's cheeks. The woman's eyes were also moist with tears. As they held each other, I leaned forward and said, "you must be husband and wife." They nodded.

I asked about the work they were doing. He said, "my wife has done the research on our family members and that is what we are doing here today; but little did I know that the first person I would baptize her for would be my own dear mother who died a year ago today." He could not control his emotions as he thought about the door that had been opened to his precious, sweet mother. How in all the world can we thank the great God enough for His plan of having temples to do this sacred work.

A wonderful sister was promised blessings as she faithfully attended the temple. She shared with me that she was driving her car through a busy intersection when a man in a pick-up truck came barreling through. Apparently, he did not see her. She told me, "I watched as the engine of his car passed right through my engine." And yet there was no collision. She proceeded on her way to the temple. She had been spared through a miracle. Blessings come from worshiping in the temple. No power on this earth can do that, but God can.

One morning, I was in the temple at about 4:30 a.m. There were only one or two other people there that early, possibly security personnel. I went to the fourth floor where the solemn assembly room is located. I unlocked the door and walked in, and as I did so, the hair on the back of my neck stood out. I had spiritual chills all over my body. I knew I was not alone. I did not see anyone or anything, but I knew there were beings from the other side of the veil that were there.

I said out loud, "I can't see you but I know you are here. If you helped build this magnificent temple, thank you, we will love you forever. I know your work; this temple will stand through the millennium. If you are here for some other reason for which God has permitted your presence here, I love you. I know you love the temple as we do. Thanks for whatever you have done or for whatever reason you are here. I will love you forever."

I was there about 20 minutes and the spiritual thrill or ecstasy which I felt did not leave until I left the solemn assembly room and the door closed behind my back, nor did the hair on the back of my neck lay down until I was out of the room and the door closed. Whoever was in the solemn assembly room with me prayed to Elohim, the same God and Father that I prayed to. I will not ever again in life neglect the marvelous love, adoration, spiritual relationship which I feel toward our Heavenly Father.

As Job was wont to exclaim, these are "things too wonderful for me" (Job 42:3).

Glorify the Father

We have in our Primary children's hymnal a song called "A Child's Prayer." The lyrics of this song are most beautiful to me. They are simple enough for a child to comprehend, yet filled with priceless information that every child needs to know as he or she grows up:

Heavenly Father, are you really there?
And do you hear and answer ev'ry child's prayer?
Some say that heaven is far away,
But I feel it close around me as I pray.
Heavenly Father I remember now
Something that Jesus told disciples long ago:
"Suffer the children to come to me."
Father, in prayer I'm coming now to thee.

Pray, he is there; Speak, he is list'ning.
You are his child; His love now surrounds you.
He hears your prayer; He loves the children.
Of such is the kingdom, the kingdom of heav'n.

As we mature, our spiritual focus seems to direct itself more towards the Savior. And, surely, this pleases the Father. There are several accounts where the grand and great Elohim witnesses "Behold my Beloved Son, in whom I am well pleased" (see 3 Nephi 11:7, also Matt. 3:17 and Mark 1:11). But we must never forget the simple faith of our children when they pray to the Father.

There is a wonderful verse in Romans chapter 15, verse 6. It states: "That ye may with one mind and one mouth glorify God, even the Father of our Lord Jesus Christ." All we do in this life, all we say with our "mouth," should glorify God.

The incomparable Christ is, as in all things, our greatest exemplar in this. He received His power from the Father and never failed to glorify Him. He testified "the son can do nothing of himself, but what he seeth the Father do: for what things soever he doeth, these also doeth the Son likewise" (John 5:19). He bears a similar witness in John 8:28: "Then said Jesus unto them, When ye have lifted up the Son of man, then shall ye know that I am he, and that I do nothing of myself; but as my Father hath taught me, I speak these things."

Throughout His teachings, the Savior constantly reminds us of the Father—our spiritual Father and His literal physical father. Again in His absolute divine love for the Father he states, "And he that sent me is with me: the Father hath not left me alone; for I do always those things that please him" (John 8:29). This is a model or pattern for us all. We need to have uppermost in our minds and hearts to do those things that please our Heavenly Father.

This is why we dress properly when we participate in priesthood ordinances. It is why we humble ourselves and submit to His will. In our clumsiness we may not remember to do everything, but we can surely prepare to the best of our knowledge and ability when we are called upon to administer to the sick. Every elder who has this privilege knows that we ourselves have no power to heal save it be by our great God in Heaven. This power which we receive when we receive the Melchizedek Priesthood only functions when we are pure in heart, submissive to God's grand will, humble enough to listen to the Spirit, and faithful enough to know that our God is a God of miracles. It may take fasting and prayer to prepare us properly. We should, when possible, be dressed in our suits, white shirts and ties. We must do our part to prepare.

The saints who desire blessings from us have pure and great faith that we are clean vessels of the Lord and that He will hear our prayers and blessings and grant them. Sometimes they have more faith in us that we do in ourselves.

Recently, President and Sister Gordon B. Hinckley came to the temple in Logan for a special Christmas devotional with the temple officiators, sealers and workers. All of the stake presidents in the entire temple district were also gathered in this special meeting in the solemn assembly room. The Prophet's visit was in itself a very special blessing, but he also left a prophetic blessing on the temple district that day.

President Hinckley's beloved companion, Marjorie Pay Hinckley, was with him. It was one of the last times she made a public appearance before her death on April 6, 2004. She was radiant. Her every act and word filled those of us who were near her with delight. She had invited Sister Featherstone to be with her and assist as was needed. This was one of the most wonderful opportunities of my wife's life. Sister Hinckley was so kind, so light hearted and filled with the Spirit that it was as though there were a special aura of light and love surrounding her.

We sent a bouquet of "talking roses" home with her and President Hinckley. There were pictures of them individually and together on the rose petals; other roses had their names and pictures of the Logan Temple. President Hinckley called the day after his visit and commented on the roses and we knew then that Sister Hinckley had loved them as she has always loved everything that is beautiful.

Everything about their visit was memorable. But it was the Prophet's blessing that had the most lasting impact. The full influence of his blessing on the temple district may not be known completely for years to come. But some of the things that have already happened are so remarkable that they could only have come about through his divine appointment.

We can predict that this will be the greatest tithing contribution year ever in the temple district. We raised the bar for missionary service and we are certain that "collectively" the greatest missionaries that have ever gone into the field from this temple district went during this year.

In the spring, the many farmers who officiated or came to the temple would often ask, "What can we do about our crops this year? We run our hands through the soil and it is dust. How do you plant in dust?"

We responded, "You must plant. President Hinckley left a blessing on this temple district."

One farmer who grows potatoes despaired. "Fertilizer for that many acres is so expensive. Bear Lake is at its lowest point in years. We can't depend on it for water. And there are other great costs. The drought is getting worse each year."

We said, "Plant your potatoes. The Prophet blessed our temple district."

The following fall we received reports from all around. The granaries in Grace, Idaho, were filled to overflowing. They shipped grain to Pocatello and filled their granaries as well as in Soda Springs. The potato crop was huge. When the water was really needed, the rains came. When the weather needed to cool down, it did. The first cutting of alfalfa was the heaviest tonnage per acre in many years. The corn silos were filled to overflowing. The cattle had a marvelous year of grazing.

The saints poured into the Logan Temple to show their appreciation. They came in Thanksgiving—or, as I like to call it, Thanks*living*—that God would be so generous in responding to His prophet's blessing on the communities in this temple district. They commented on Sister Hinckley and her sweetness during the visit.

We had over an increase of over 100% in endowments performed in the temple that fall. We are confident that the saints will continue this marvelous temple work out of gratitude. President Hinckley blessed us by his visit and all of us bless his holy and great name and his prophetic call as prophet, seer and revelator.

The entire temple district—every ward and branch, every coordinating group and sealing group in the temple—sang at least once during the month, "We Ever Pray For Thee":

We ever pray for thee, our prophet dear,
That God will give to thee comfort and cheer;
As the advancing years furrow thy brow,
Still may the light within shine bright as now,
Still may the light within shine bright as now.

We ever pray for thee with all our hearts,
That strength be given thee to do thy part,
To guide and counsel us from day to day,
To shed a holy light around our way,
To shed a holy light around our way.

We ever pray for thee with fervent love;
And as the children's prayer is heard above,
Thou shalt be ever blest, and God will give
All that is meet and best while thou shalt live,
All that is meet and best while thou shalt live.

Yes, President Hinckley, "We ever pray for thee with fervent love...as the children's prayer is heard above." How do we express our love to a God who not only provides His Son as our Redeemer and Savior of the world; and who gives us temples for our blessing and endowment; but also blesses our lives with holy prophets of God. Always He has given us His prophets to lead, guide, direct, and bless our lives.

No wonder we dress in our best when we are called upon to administer to the sick. In our need for guidance and direction we are approaching the throne of the most high God. I am sure it pleases Him to know we have cleansed our bodies, dressed properly and humbled ourselves in total submission to give the blessing He would have us give. Our prophets set the fine example of these principles.

Years ago I was in Reno, Nevada, and a Bishop said, "do you see President Kimball often?" I responded that I did. He asked me to give President Kimball a message from him. He said, "President Kimball came to our stake five years ago. My wife and I had been married for a lengthy period of time and had not been able to have any children. I asked President Kimball to give a blessing of healing to my wife." He continued, "In the five years since we have had five children." Then he said smiling, "Could you ask President Kimball to call off the blessing now?"

Such life-changing blessings are preceded by much prayer, faith and preparation. Then a call is made to one of the Lord's servants to administer. We submit ourselves to the will of the Father. Our Father knows our needs. He knows our hearts. And we should be willing to accept His divine will whether the answer be "Yes, you can be healed," "no, not at this time," or even "not in this life." We are all in the hands of a loving Father, and if we have faith in Him, we will accept His will and know that it is for our good in the eternities to come.

A Father's Prayer

God is a personal God who understands all of His children and their frustrations, trials and anxieties—even frustrations that may seem trivial in the grand scheme of things. He is an attentive Father. Truly his "tender mercies" are over us (see 1 Nephi 1:21).

In the late seventies, while I was the Young Men's General President, I was asked to serve as the commissary chairman at a National Jamboree for the Boy Scouts of America. The chief scout executive had asked President Monson for approval to have me do it and President Monson approved it. Two things happened for which I will ever be grateful. The first was that Latter-day Saint scouters from all over America volunteered to serve with me in the commissary. One third of the 765 staff were members of the

Church. Other jamborees, there had only been a handful of Latter-day Saints that worked in the commissary.

The second miracle was that a kind Heavenly Father inspired me when I needed His heavenly guidance. As commissary chairman, I was responsible for preparing approximately one million meals in ten days. One of my direct responsibilities was to raise $250,000.00 of food in kind. This was to help offset the high cost of the Jamboree. When I learned of this responsibility, I sat in my office and pondered. I had been an executive with a large grocery chain; but approximately fifteen years had passed since I had been involved in the grocery business. I had few contacts left in the industry and I felt overwhelmed. I sat in the office and offered a heart-felt prayer to God as to how I should go about doing this. I finished praying, sat at the desk and the answer came, something I never had considered. I was to contact the chief executive officers of major grocery companies and appeal to them of a contribution.

I wrote a letter to Publix Food in Florida and asked them how they would like to contribute all the fruit juice, orange juice, oranges and grapefruit, etc. I said the contribution would be equal to about $25,000 cash. In two weeks I received a check for $25,000 made out to the Boy Scouts of America. I contacted Robert Bolinbroke from Kingsford Charcoal Corp. and asked how they would like to contribute part or all of the charcoal for the whole Jamboree.

They responded in a few days that they would contribute it all which as I recall was equivalent to about $55,000. All we needed to so was to put a sign on all the stacks of charcoal letting scouts and scouters, visitors, know that it was a contribution from this great organization. They contributed the total amount and delivered it all the way to Fort A.P. Hill Virginia for us for free. I asked Darold Johnson if he would see if Kraft Cheese would contribute cheese. We received a $65,000 dollar gift. Sam Skaggs during a single phone call agreed to furnish all the bread and English muffins. Dan Gardiner, owner of Dan's grocery stores, Albertsons, Smith's Food King and other organizations contributed generously in cash equivalent to the value of the products we asked them to contribute: peanut butter, preserves, condiments, pancake flour, syrup, etc. The money and goods came pouring in. In all, we raised over $335,000 in cash and food in kind.

When it was all raised I looked back and considered how a wise Father had inspired me. I was the Young Men's General President, an Area President over the Southeast and the Caribbean. I was the Chairman of the Church Scouting Committee and on several other Church committees. My responsibilities were pressing. And yet my Church callings were not impaired one particle by the special assignment I had received. Raising all that money turned out to be a fairly simple task. The BSA organization was satisfied. The only criticism I received was when they ran out of coffee one night and someone sent word back to leadership that it was because a "Mormon" was the commissary chairman.

Four years later, I was a chaplain at the National Jamboree for the Boy Scouts of America. I had just attended the Canadian National Jamboree on Prince Edward Island. I spent several days there then went to Montreal where I spoke to a regional group of youth. Next I traveled to Kitchner and another youth conference before making my way to Toronto for a third group. I left there and went straight to Fort A.P. Hill, Virginia, where I commenced my duties as a chaplain for the National BSA Jamboree.

I was pretty tired when I got there and things only got worse. I was assigned to a large tent that housed about 30 scout leaders. We were on wooden cots covered with canvas. They were narrow and my shoulders touched the sides. They were approximately six feet long so I just barely fit lengthwise. The hours were long and the many activities were strenuous. By the second week at the Jamboree (my third week away from home), I was exhausted. But I was having trouble sleeping. It was August in Virginia. The temperature felt to be about 100 degrees at night and the humidity was nearly 100%. The mosquitoes were swarming, so you had to keep covered. I would go to bed with a thin blanket over me, despite the heat, and usually wouldn't be able to drift off until about midnight.

One night, I was visited with the most remarkable dream. I was with my wife in the most beautiful place with the most exquisite feelings I have ever had. The dream lasted for some time. I awakened and pondered on this wonderful experience. Then I fell back to sleep and the dream continued. I think I have some small understanding of what the celestial kingdom will be like because this particular dream was so glorious and filled with love.

When I awakened in the morning I had the supreme feeling that the service I was rendering—the long time away from home in such miserable conditions—was recognized by a loving Father. God appreciated the supposed sacrifice I was making and He somehow knew that I needed such an experience. I think I felt closer to my wife after that dream than I ever had before, and she was hundreds of miles away. Only God, to whom I prayed each night before going to bed, could know what I was feeling. And only He could bring the sweetness and the refreshment that this dream brought me.

At that same National Jamboree, I had another singular experience with prayer. Our son Paul was able to go to Fort A.P. Hill as a patrol leader. I was at the Jamboree before his troop arrived. And when he came, I tried to break loose and was able to have a meal or two with him.

One night after dinner he said, "Dad, can you please come and watch our patrol go through the challenge course?" I was so busy and the demands on my time were great. I said, "I'll try Paul but it looks doubtful." I asked when they were going to the challenge (obstacle) course. I said I'd try.

The next morning I went to my post early and was able to get someone to fill in for me for an hour. My intention was to find Paul, but on the way to the challenge course I must have seen 5,000 boys, and that is a conservative estimate. They were all dressed in the oldest, most ragged clothing they had. The BSA had recommended that they wear clothes that could be thrown away after negotiating the obstacles. But the effect was that they all looked alike. I don't think I could have recognized Paul if I had looked right at him, and I knew I couldn't wait for him. I went to the course and asked the scouter posted there if I could come in and watch a patrol go through the course. He responded "Elder Featherstone, you are on the executive board of BSA. You can go anywhere."

I thought I could at least tell Paul that I saw the obstacle course and walked through with a patrol, so he would know I had made the effort. The scouter at the gate pointed me down the trail to the beginning post where the patrols started and proceeded through a very tough, muddy and rugged course. A patrol was waiting and would be the next one to go through. As I approached, I was startled to find that it was Paul's patrol. Out of the thousands of patrols there that day, his was the one ready for the course when I arrived.

Coincidence? No way. By chance? Almost impossible. It was a miracle. I can't describe the expression on Paul's face when he saw me. I'm sure he thought I was not going to be able to make it. I remember thinking, *God did this for me. He knows I have spent almost my entire adult life before and after being called as a General Authority working with the youth. I have not withheld any energy in trying to be for the youth what it was God wanted me to be and so He has blessed me to be with my son this day.* I cannot number the youth conferences, encampments, firesides, morningsides, speaking engagements, Eagle Court of Honors, Philmont Mormon Week assignments, and the like that I have attended, but they were all worth it to know that my Father in Heaven was aware of my service and had blessed me in a time of personal need.

Would you just think it through with me for a minute? The great God in Heaven, with all the realms over which He presides, the myriads of souls on this earth and in His other kingdoms, somehow heard the prayer of a lowly servant who had turned to Him and pled with heart and soul for a simple blessing. And in His great majesty, He found a way to answer the prayer of my heart. In other chapters, we have discussed His omnipotence and omniscience. Possibly this is an example of His omnipresence in our lives. He is God and nothing—not anything—is too hard for Him. He is even mindful of the little things.

We all ought to feel a sense of security, peace and love knowing that we are His children and He loves us all with the unconditional, eternal love of a Father...our Father.

The Compassion of Our Father in Heaven

One of the Father's most persistent characteristics is his compassion for His children. In the Topical Guide under the word "compassion," it suggests "see also benevolence; charity; comfort; God, love of; kindness; mercy; pity; welfare." One thing we can be sure of is that in the most trying moments of our lives, He will be there.

In a revelation to the Prophet Joseph, the Savior brought peace with these comforting words "And now the year of my redeemed is come; and they shall mention the loving kindness of their Lord, and all that he has bestowed upon them according to his goodness, and according his loving kindness, forever and ever" (D&C 133:52). Yet the loving kindness of the Savior is itself modeled on the Father's loving kindness. The Savior gives us a grand key in John when He states, "I say unto you, The Son can do nothing of himself, but what he seeth the Father do: for what things soever he doeth, these also doeth the Son likewise" (John 5:19).

A wonderful young father once borrowed a substantial amount of money from a dear friend. He borrowed the money to make a sizeable purchase overseas on behalf of one of his clients. A contract had been agreed to, the foreign product bought and paid for, but when the products arrived complications set in. The fine young man went to the buyer to make the delivery only to find the purchasing agent had been replaced and the newly appointed officer was not willing to honor the previous man's agreement. The young man was desperate. It could ruin him financially. He turned to a God of love and fasted and prayed for three days and nights. Eventually, the heart of the new purchasing agent was softened and he agreed to accept the product. It was God's loving kindness for a young man who was "pure in heart" that brought an answer to his desperate prayer.

I had the pleasure of visiting the Bloomfield Hills Michigan Stake several times on Church assignment. This is the stake where the late George Romney lived and had presided at one time. I loved and respected that man so much that I called on him to speak each time I visited. It was a self-indulgence for me and a great blessing to the people.

One Sunday night I had a fireside scheduled just outside of Detroit. I asked the mission president whether he thought George Romney would be there. He said "Its my understanding that he is in Washington D.C." Brother Romney headed up the national "volunteerism" program at the time. That night, just before the meeting started, I went into the chapel and Brother Romney and his wonderful companion, Lenore, were on about the third row back on the side. I went down off the stand to greet one of my great heroes. He said some very kind things to me and about me. Someone once said, "Compliments are not what we are but what we should be." I wanted to be what he said I was.

Before I went back up on the stand I felt a sweep of inspiration, I said "Brother Romney, usually I have you speak, how would you feel if I had Lenore speak tonight." I can't tell you how pleased he was. They were both in their eighties. When I called on her she was just a little unsteady making her way to the pulpit. As soon as she took hold of both sides of the pulpit she seemed dramatically energized. I would like to share all that she said because it was beautiful and a magnificent tribute to her husband. She bore witness to all that I had loved and admired about him. Then she shared a very tender personal story that I will never forget.

She was expecting a baby, her last child, when complications set in with the pregnancy. There was some serious bleeding, and the doctor was not sure the baby would survive. She said something like "my blessed husband, George, went into a period of fasting and prayer. He fasted and prayed four days and nights." Then out of the far realms of heaven this great man's faith, fasting and prayer were rewarded. She had a healthy son. They named him Mitt. He has grown into a faithful man of God in his own right. I have come to love and respect Mitt Romney as I did his father. The first time I met Mitt, I looked at this handsome, square-jawed man—the miracle his father, George, had prayed for—and felt the same deep abiding love for him that I felt for his father.

God the Father is kind and deals with His children as a loving Father would. The mercy and benevolence of God are from eternity to eternity. These blessings come as part of the great plan of happiness—the faith part.

Years ago as a fairly young father, I took my wife to the hospital to have our fifth child. Shortly after we arrived at the hospital, it became clear that things were not progressing as they should. I was very concerned and it seemed to me that the doctor was also worried. He examined my wife often. He came in toward the end, listened to the baby's heart with a stethoscope and then turned and asked me to leave. I went out of her room, walked 30 or 40 steps down the hall, and looked out the south window of the maternity ward. I started praying for my wife and our unborn son.

All of a sudden I heard her door open. A nurse ran out. She ran down the hall and dragged an oxygen tank back to my wife's room. She rushed in and closed the door behind her. I cannot describe in words the desperation that I felt at that moment. I thought I had been praying, but in an instant, my prayers seemed a thousand times more intense. I was standing at the window looking out. Tears were streaming down my cheeks. We had four sons and I remember promising God that I would try to do everything he wanted me to do. I committed in that desperate hour to spend my life serving Him. I would do what He wanted me to do and more, I would be what He wanted me to be and more and I would go wherever in the world He would have me go. I remember my total and absolute commitment no matter what the outcome. I suppose I had prayed deeply and meaningfully before that night over other deep concerns; but that night I knew that I was absolutely dependent on Him.

It seemed like a forever moment until the doctor wheeled my wife out of her room to the delivery room. It seemed ages before he reappeared and said, "Vaughn, you have a fine 10 lb. 12 oz. baby boy. Your wife is fine."

Had someone asked me at that moment how much I loved God, I would not have been able to utter a word, but I knew it would be with my total soul. And those feelings have not changed in all the years since then.

We have many who go through similarly dark and terrible trials and sometimes lives are not spared or conditions do not change.

It takes an absolute trust in a loving and kind Father in Heaven who has ten thousand times more compassion than we have to accept such outcomes. I have known since the night mentioned above that if the answer had been different, my love and faith in God would not have changed.

He has perfect compassion. He knows the heartrending problems that are part of life. We are all tested, driven to our knees, humbled to the dust of the earth. We need to trust in His loving kindness that what happens is in His grand design for us. We must bow in reverence and submission to His will and be willing to accept it no matter how difficult the trial.

I recently memorized a poem that reflects in verse what I have attempted to state.

My Life is But a Weaving

My life is but a weaving between my God and me
I do not choose the colors, yet he worketh steadily
Ofttimes he weaveth sorrow, and I in foolish pride
Forget he sees the upper and I the under side.
Not til the loom is silent and the shuttles cease to fly
Will he undo the canvas and reveal the reasons why
The dark treads were as needful in the skillful weaver's hand
As the threads of gold and silver in the pattern he had planned.

He is the master weaver and will make a beautiful tapestry of our lives if we are submissive.

For eight years Elder Maxwell suffered and continued to bless God's holy name. What an example to the saints everywhere. Elder Haight nearly lost his life due to a very serious heart condition, returned from near death to bless the Church.

President Hinckley, wonderful, beloved prophet shared the feeling of loss and loneliness since his eternal companion's passing.

Coming to know the compassionate nature of our Father in Heaven helps us to humbly and submissively say "Father, thy will be done" in our own lives and then trust in Him.

I know now that had I been killed in the accident my wife and I went through, I could have accepted that decision. We are in His hands and that is the safest place to be through the eternities.

The Love of "Father"

In the realms where God the Eternal Father dwells, we see the purity of perfection. Our God and Father is perfect without one particle of a flaw. His will is consistent with His perfect example, doctrine, eternal principles and all absolute truth. He never does vary from perfection and will not through the eternities. His will is perfection for each one of us. His condescension is to visit us in our weakness and spiritual infirmities. It is to provide each of us with His glorious confidence that by and by we can become like Him and be joint heirs with His Only Begotten.

There is a divine probing spirit that is a constant reminder of his love to those who are anxious to follow Him. His love rests upon our souls and prompts us to do those things that will bring joy, peace, contentment, and happiness on our walk through life.

Shouldn't we then bless the lives of those around us? We ought to be the supreme blessing in the lives of our families, husbands, wives, mothers, fathers and children. Those of us who are recently married, or those who are in the golden, crowning years of our lives, should of spiritual necessity strive to be all that His wonderful plan of happiness will provide.

Sometimes I have been confronted with people who have otherwise been faithful but who grieve because their last words to their loved one in mortality were spoken in anger. It is spiritual immaturity for some who have had angry discussions, serious conflicts, or heated words with a loved spouse, son or daughter to suppose that those negative destructive feelings carry into the spirit world. With death all those feelings melt away as the hoar frost. They are nothing and should not be retained in our thoughts for one negative moment.

At death only the sweetest, kindest, most sentimental and holy thoughts survive in the lives of saints who have tried to do the best they can. We should and will receive that sweet peace that whispers tender thoughts of love and caring and removes the harsh and bitter words we may have spoken when overwrought or frustrated. With God our Father, what we really are and what we are striving to become is what matters; not some temporary flash of words spoken out of anger or impertinence, although we need to control and master them. My counsel to such brothers and sisters is to cast all negative remembrances about your loved one off forever and remember them with tenderness and love.

We would do well to heed that same advice while our loved ones are yet living. Our Father in Heaven expects us to remove prickly problems that come in marriage. Bickering, nagging, complaining and finding fault are attitudes that need to be modified. The Lord commands us to "love one another, as I have loved you" (John 15:12). This is especially true in marriage. Love, forgive, soften, increase tenderness, remember the Father of us all wants us to be happy. Focus on the beautiful, positive traits in your spouse.

Our spiritual Father is surely pleased when we see our companion through rose-colored glasses. Truly we ought to be each other's best friend. We ought to focus on what is most beautiful and handsome in each other. The images of the past, if negative, can be overshadowed with renewed love and feelings for each other. Rose-colored glasses filter out the unlovely, the critical, the negative, the unkind mistakes, the sins and transgressions, and view present things as they are. How delicious and wonderful to have a love that is so precious and so dear that it pleases a kind and loving Father. With God's great help, no power on earth or in hell, no influence of the evil one can penetrate the haven of love of a righteous, God-fearing, commandment-living couple.

Bring spring to your marriage over and over again with love and kindness, thoughtfulness and effort, and love truly can blossom brilliantly over and over and over again. Even mature rosebushes can blossom more beautifully as the years pass when they are properly pruned, watered and cared for. Mature marriages, in a similar fashion, bloom even more brilliantly and with sweeter fragrance as the years pass on.

The wonderful thing about mature marriages is that husbands and wives are surrounded by so many memories of shared experiences together. It would seem consistent that the Father of our spirits would have us use our magnificent memories to relive the most wonderful times in our marriage. Memory can take us trailing back to special occasions—the birth of a child, a miraculous answer to prayer, family vacations, past expressions of love that have become indelible moments when everything seemed perfect, achievements in satisfying each other or of truly becoming one. We need our memories to bring back vividly the seasons of pleasure, moments of compassion, hours of special relationship experiences and years of togetherness. Memory is a God-created blessing in the lives of those who are good and who want to please God. His love is eternal, endless and all-encompassing and it is without end.

We know our Father in Heaven lives. He is Elohim, the Father of our spirits. He has created worlds without number. Myriads of His spiritual children bear sacred witness that His work and glory is to "bring to pass the immortality and eternal life" of mankind (Moses 1:39).

Obedience to God, following His glorious direction and teaching as laid down in the Gospel of Jesus Christ, is the only path leading to a fullness of joy in our marriages and in our devotion to each other.

Let us resolve today that with the love of our Father in Heaven, and through the example of His Son, home can truly be a heaven on earth and a marriage relationship can be the most pleasurable and blessed of all unions. We must all remember that God the Eternal Father and our Eternal Mother will bring us back home to be theirs forever and to have that perfect relationship with each other as they have, if we strive toward a perfect relationship and a total commitment to keep His commandments.

Dennis and Carol Flake have been a marvelous example to me of the guidance and direction our Heavenly Parent is anxious to give His offspring if we will let Him. Dennis and Carol have both passed on, but what a legacy they have left for their children through faithful living.

I was released as a Stake President of the Boise North Stake when I was called to serve as a General Authority. At the same Stake Conference, Elder Mark E. Petersen divided the Stake. The new stake was the Meridian Idaho Stake. I was invited to nominate to Elder Petersen a worthy brother to serve as a patriarch. My thoughts immediately went to Dennis Flake. After going through the process and feeling at peace with the Spirit I recommended that Elder Petersen consider Brother Flake. He had served in a Stake Presidency and as a Bishop and had always been a wonderful Priesthood leader. Elder Petersen called Dennis Flake to serve as the Stake Patriarch.

Brother Flake and his wife had been missionaries with Elder Bruce R. McConkie. Elder McConkie was, in fact, the one who had suggested that Carol, then Sister Reid, would make a wonderful wife for Dennis. Dennis met her and, after returning home, they courted and married.

My wife and I first met the Flakes when we went to Boise in 1956. They had a large family. In one of our first sacrament meetings there, one of their sons, Lawrence, spoke and quoted the entire 4th section of the Doctrine and Covenants:

> *Now behold, a marvelous work is about to come forth among the children of men.*
>
> *Therefore, O ye that embark in the service of God, see that ye serve him with all your heart, might, and mind and strength, that ye may stand blameless before God at the last day.*
>
> *Therefore, if ye have desires to serve God ye are called to the work;*
>
> *For behold the field is white already to harvest; and lo, he that thrusteth in his sickle with his might, the same layeth up in store that he perisheth not, but bringeth salvation to his soul;*
>
> *And faith, hope, charity and love, with an eye single to the glory of God, qualify him for the work.*

Remember faith, virtue, knowledge, temperance, patience, brotherly kindness, godliness, charity, humility, diligence.

Ask, and ye shall receive; knock, and it shall be opened unto you. Amen. (D&C 4:1–7)

He not only quoted it, but I could tell by the way he spoke the words that he believed it. The Flakes had their entire family memorize the 4th section. We were so impressed with the idea that we appropriated it for our family. I was a young twenty-five-year-old father of at the time. All six of our sons memorized Section 4. I believe our daughter did also.

The 4th section is the great missionary scripture. Most missions have their missionaries quote it at zone conferences. It is quoted at the missionary training center on a regular basis. I believe that scripture has had a great impact on those who commit it to memory.

The Flake boys all served missions and were totally obedient. They all became leaders in the mission field. They have all married and gone on to perform great acts of service in the Church. Their sons and daughters have all made magnificent contributions to the Church. Joel Flake was a Stake President and a Mission President when I served as President of the Northeast Area. Dennis and Lawrence have become two of my dearest friends.

When Dennis was called to serve his first mission in Australia, he served in the mission over which Bruce R.

McConkie presided. I was invited to speak at his "farewell." I drove to Boise, spoke at the sacrament meeting and drove part way back to Salt Lake Sunday night. The next morning as I was back on the road I heard a news flash from Boise that the residence of Dennis and Carol Flake had burned to the ground. I was shocked. Apparently the fire had started from a welding torch that was being used to thaw frozen pipes. The house and its contents were a total loss. I got to a phone and called the Bishop and said, "I guess Dennis won't be going on his mission." The Bishop was emotional when he said, "I talked to Brother and Sister Flake and they said, 'Dennis is going on his mission. He will be at the mission home in Salt Lake this week when he is supposed to be there.'"

From the Flake boys there have been three full-time mission presidents, one Regional Representative, two stake presidents (I think), three members of stake presidencies, bishops, one chaplain in the military and all have been wonderful priesthood leaders as have the husbands of the Flake girls. Four of the brothers are with the Church Education System. Lawrence is a professor of Religion at BYU. Dennis, Joel and Forest have all made major contributions to Institute and Seminary. Lane is the U.S. Chaplain.

The daughter Carol is just like her mother a wonderful, committed mother and dedicated Latter-Day Saint. I am sure this is true of the other daughters. The other brothers are all active and totally dedicated.

The Flakes did it as well as it can be done. The parents left a financial legacy that is continually contributed to in order to assist grandchildren and great grandchildren to go on missions.

Our Father in Heaven must be pleased with parents who teach and train their children to be obedient and responsive to the Spirit. In a far greater way the Father of us all has that special interest in each one of us so that we might be as the Flakes have been, instruments in His holy hands to perform His work.

What a contrast are parents who misguide or let their children wander spiritually because they themselves have never found spiritual stability.

Our Father in Heaven must be very pleased with Dennis and Carol Flake and all the parents like them who have made serving God and teaching their children their chief joy in life. I think if we could have an interview with father Dennis, he would say, "I have tried to do it the way I think our Father in Heaven would do it." Father in Heaven would surely not leave us without a plan to enable us to come back into His presence.

Father in Heaven has given us a program of direction for raising a family and bringing them back home to Him. They are His children and He has entrusted them in our care. We are accountable to Him for each one entrusted to our care. Success in our family will be far greater if we follow the pattern of divine parents—Dennis and Carol Flake did this.

To my knowledge every son and daughter married in the temple. Every son and every grandson and great grandson have all gone on missions. What more eternal reward could we ask. The Flakes will make a marvelous contribution collectively to this wonderful Church, God's Church, The Church of Jesus Christ of Latter-day Saints. God help us to follow His holy and divine pattern of parenthood.

A Tribute to God's Prophets

The attached is a poem dedicated to the Prophet Joseph Smith and President Gordon B. Hinckley. The prophetic direction to build the Nauvoo Temple was inspired. The saints gave their all to fulfill the commands of the Lord to build His holy house.

They had seen the Kirtland Temple desecrated shortly after it was dedicated. John A. Widtsoe, who had a special feeling about temples and was told he would in his patriarchal blessing, made a statement that if you compare the cost of building the Kirtland Temple to the principle of the "widow's mite," the temple cost more to build than any building up to that time.

God's holy prophets build temples. Holiness to God the Father and Holiness to the Lord Jesus Christ. We build them to honor the Father and the Son and to do the most holy work in them.

This poem was written about a year before the Nauvoo Temple dedication and reflects my feelings about the "new" and "old" Nauvoo temples.

We will build temples as long as man is found on the earth in its present state.

Nauvoo, The Beautiful's Holy House
Elder Vaughn J. Featherstone, October 26, 2000

They drained a swamp and found a home
On Mississippi's friendly banks.
They called this holy place Nauvoo,
In reverence bowed and gave their thanks.
Then Joseph as our prophet seer
With towering faith and solemn prayer
Announced a temple would be built
To bind eternal's blessings there.

Great and mighty, men of faith
With hands huge, and calloused through
Would build this temple strong and great
A millennium to stand...or two.
When this precious work was done
A holy house for God there'd be
An ensign to the latter Saints.
And bless them for eternity.

Vaughn J. Featherstone

Like ancient pyramids of old
  And China's wall both bleak and bare
The temple in Nauvoo would stand,
  Would cleft the sky and rend the air
Built with faith and hope and love
  Built with stone and grateful tears
The symbol of their love for God
  To stand supreme a thousand years.

This beacon of their love and faith
  A holy house His Son could own
Heavenward it lifted day by day
  More grand it stood, more light it shone.
With star and moon and sunstone too,
  Erect, magnificent and bold
It rose to prominence in those days
  More precious than rubies, jewels, and gold.

Then bad men came with satanic flames
  And torched the temple to the ground
The prophets grieved and angels wept
  While the flock of Saints did gather round.
Then great winds stirred and whipped and lashed
  The walls then tumbled to the earth.
The jewel of all the Saints possessed
  Was leveled low, soon after birth.

One hundred fifty years and six
    Another prophet with vision clear,
Would dedicate another temple in Nauvoo
    To Christ the Lord whom we revere.
The finest work that could be done
    Has built this temple grander far
And future Saints will marvel yet
    The temple of the Morning Star.

Then He whose work this temple is
    Shall harbor faithful Saints once more
For lo Nauvoo this garden fair
    Will be as lovely as before.
And though a thousand years shall pass
    When hearts grow faint and dim,
This monument to our God will stand
    A sacred temple built for Him.

Then God will crown this noble place
    While ancient prophets visit here
They'll marvel at this wondrous work
    And sing the songs that we revere.
How beautiful in heaven, are the feet
    Washed clean with tears of gratitude
For those whose work will now be done
    Who wait in quiet, solemn mood.

I have composed the following verses about our God and Father. They line up with the doctrine of the supreme God in heaven and earth, the Father of us all and great architect of the plan of salvation and happiness.

The Grand and Gracious Elohim
Vaughn J. Featherstone, April 16, 2003

Beyond the earth, the moon and stars
*   Our Father Elohim resides.*
His throne on Kolob governs all
*   Across the galaxies He strides.*
All dominion, power and might are His
*   His myriad seed He watches o'er*
He gave His Son as sacrifice
*   That we may dwell with Him once more.*

He governs the world, the Kokaubeam
*   And in eternal splendor rules*
All earth and heaven worship Him
*   Supreme His love, salvation's tools.*
The glorious Father of us all
*   Salvation's plan He deigned to be*
That His immortal offspring live
*   With Him through all eternity.*

On "The Last Drop in the Chalice" by Victor Hugo

Vaughn J. Featherstone, March 1, 2003

From Heaven there comes to each and all
    trials great and trials small.
So oft the tears of sorrow flow
    we suffer another heart sick blow
We see our image in the glass
    and then we wonder as we pass,
Is this the last drop in the chalice
    consigned to dwell in tent or palace.

We wander heartsick in a daze
    and contemplate how long it stays;
And whether we will rack with pain
    to humanize our lives again.
These sands of life sift through the glass
    while minutes, days and hours pass
On the anvil we lie and wait
    For one last blow if that's our fate.

All suffering we go through here below
    comes individually and we grow;
Then finally when ought else is left
    through fervent prayer the heavens cleft
And He who hears the smallest prayer
    confirms that He is always there
We'll enter His celestial palace
    Having drunk the last drop in the chalice.

Untitled

Vaughn J. Featherstone, August 21, 2003

Thou gracious father, who nourisheth all
  Have mercy on us when we fall
Hide thine eyes from failures sore
  Let us try once more, once more.
For thou who judgest great and small
  Remember us the least of all
Give new hope, new birth, new life
  Remove our sins, our tears, our strife.

May we bow and kiss thy feet
  Let us be cleansed, redeemed and sweet
For we are less than dust and sand
  Unless thou molds us in thine hand.
We'll sing the songs of angel choirs
  And worship with our harps and lyres
Redeeming blood will heal us through
  In robes of white we'll dwell with you.

"Poetry Lifts Our Spirits to God"

Poetical Writings of Orson F. Whitney—
Juvenile Instructor, 1889

Some years back in one of my books,
I received permission from the First Presidency to include
a talk given by President Spencer W. Kimball entitled
"Absolute Truth." It is a marvelous talk that we need to
review on a regular basis. President Boyd K. Packer in his
book *Teach Ye Diligently* included the marvelous talk which
President J. Reuben Clark had given regarding teaching. The
inclusion of this particular chapter is one that I think helps
us understand the majesty, the greatness, the goodness, the
omnipotence, omniscience, and omnipresence of God. This is
a poem written by Orson F. Whitney which President Boyd
K. Packer quoted at a devotional in the Logan Temple. It is
a marvelous verse and hopefully including it in this book will

make available to many people who might not have access to this marvelous, spiritually poetic tribute paid by Orson F. Whitney to the great God in Heaven.

Immanuel—A Christmas Idyl

I.

In solemn council sat the Gods;
From Kolob's height supreme,
Celestial light blazed forth afar
O'er countless kokaubeam.
And faintest tinge, the fiery fringe
Of that resplendent day,
'Lumined the dark abysmal realm
Where earth in chaos lay.

Silence self-spelled; the hour was one
When thought doth most avail;
Of worlds unborn the destiny
Hung trembling in the scale.
Silence o'er all, and there arose,
Those kings and priests among,
A Power sublime, than whom appeared
None mightier 'mid the throng.

A stature mingling strength and grace,
Of meek though Godlike mien,
The love-revealing countenance

Lustrous as lightning sheen;
Whiter his hair than ocean spray,
Or frost of alpine hill.
He spake;—attention grew more grave,
The stillness e'en more still.

"Father!"—the voice like music fell,
Clear as the murmuring flow
Of mountain streamlet, trickling down
From heights of virgin snow—
"Father!" it said, "since one must die
Thy children to redeem,
Whilst earth, as yet unformed and void,
With pulsing life shall teem;

"And thou, great Michael, foremost fall,
That mortal man may be
And chosen Saviour yet must send,
Lo, here am I—send me!
I ask, I seek no recompense,
Save that which then were mine;
Mine be the willing sacrifice,
The endless glory, Thine!"

"Give me to lead to this lorn world,
When wandered from the fold,
Twelve legions of the noble ones
That now thy face behold;

Tried souls, 'mid untried spirits found;
  That captained these may be,
And crowned the dispensations all
  With powers of Deity.

"A love that hath redeemed all worlds,
  All worlds must still redeem;
But mercy cannot justice rob—
  Or where were Elohim?
Freedom—man's faith, man's work, God's grace—
  Must span the great gulf o'er;
Life, death, the guerdon or the doom,
  Rejoice we or deplore."

Silence once more. Then sudden rose
  Aloft a towering form,
Proudly erect as lowering peak
  'Lumed by the gathering storm!
A presence bright and beautiful,
  With eye of flashing fire,
A lip whose haughty curl bespoke
  A sense of inward ire.

"Give me to go," thus boldly cried,
  With scarce concealed disdain;
"And hence shall none, from heaven to earth,
  That shall not rise again.
My saving plan exception scorns;

Man's agency unknown;
As recompense, I claim the right
To sit on yonder throne!"

Ceased Lucifer. The breathless hush
Resumed and denser grew.
All eyes were turned; the general gaze
One common magnet drew.
A moment there was solemn pause;
Then, like the thunder-burst,
Rolled forth from lips omnipotent—
From Him both last and first:

"Immanuel! thou my Messenger,
Till time's probation end.
And one shall go thy face before,
While twelve thy steps attend.
And many more, on that far shore,
The pathway shall prepare,
That I, the First, the last may come,
And earth my glory share.

"Go forth, thou chosen of the Gods,
Whose strength shall in thee dwell!
Go down betime and rescue earth,
Dethroning death and hell
On thee alone man's fate depends,
The fate of beings all.

Thou shalt not fail, though thou art free—
    Free, but too great, to fall.

"By three in heaven, by three on earth,—
    By blood that sanctifies,
By water of obedience,
    Spirit that justifies;
By every word of mine and thine,
    Through toil and travail sore,
Man, God-redeemed, with God shall be,
    As God forevermore."

'T was done. From congregation vast,
    Tumultuous murmurs rose;
Waves of conflicting sound, as when
    Two meeting seas oppose.
'T was finished. But the heavens wept;
    And still their annals tell
How one was choice of Elohim,
    O'er One who fighting fell.

II.
A stranger star that came from far,
    To fling its silver ray,
Where, cradled a lowly cave,
    A lowlier infant lay;
And led by soft sidereal light,
    The Orient sages bring

Rare gifts of gold and frankincense,
To greet the homeless King.

Oh wondrous grace! Will Gods go down
Thus low that men may rise?
Imprisoned here the mighty one
Who reigned in yonder skies?
Hark to that chime!—a tongue sublime
That tells the hour of noon;
A dying world is welcoming
Life—light of sun and moon.

"Peace! peace!"—thy voice, eternity!
"Peace!" echoes time's false tone.
"Peace! peace!" Is discord then no more?
Are earth and heaven as one?
Peace, peace, where sparkling hosts proclaim
A monarch manger-born;
There ruler of unnumbered realms,
Here throneless and forlorn.

He wandered through the faithless world,
A Prince in shepherd's guise;
He called his scattered flock, but few
The voice would recognize;
For minds upborne by hollow pride,
Or dimmed by sordid lust,
Ne'er look for kings in beggar's garb—

For diamonds in the dust.

Wept He above a city doomed,
  Her temple, walls and towers;
O'er palaces where recreant priests
  Usurped unhallowed powers.
"I am the way, the life, the light!"
  Alas! 't was heeded not;
Ignored—nay, mocked God's messenger,
  And spurned the truth He taught.

O bane of damning unbelief!
  Till now when e'er so rife?
Thou stumbling stone, thou barrier 'thwart
  The gates of endless life!
O love of self, and Mammon's lust!
  Twin portals to despair,
Where bigotry, the blinded bat,
  Flaps through the midnight air.

Through these, gloom-wrapt Gethsemane!
  Thy glens of guilty shade
Grieved o'er the sinless Son of God,
  By gold-bought kiss betrayed;
Beheld Him unresisting dragged,
  Forsaken, friendless, lone,
To halls where dark-browed hatred sat
  On judgment's lofty throne.

As sheep before His shearers, dumb,
*   Those patient lips were mute;*
The clamorous charge of taunting tongues
*   He deigned not to dispute.*
They smote with cruel palm a face
*   Which felt yet bore the sting;*
Then crowned with thorns His quivering brow,
*   And mocking, hailed him "King!"*

Transfixt He hung,—O crime of crimes!—
*   The God whom worlds adore.*
"Father, forgive them!" Drained the dregs;
*   Immanuel was no more!*
No more where thunders shook the earth,
*   Where lightnings, 'thwart the gloom,*
Saw that unconquered spirit spurn
*   The shackles of the tomb.*

Far-flashing on its wings of light,
*   A falchion from its sheath,*
It cleft the realms of darkness and
*   Dissolved the bands of death;*
Hell's dungeons burst, wide open swung
*   The everlasting bars,*
Whereby the ransomed soul shall win
*   Those heights beyond the stars.*

Following are excerpts from Elder Whitney's chapter on Poets and Poetry. God the Father has been generous in giving talents and spiritual gifts to the prophets and apostles and others who elevate the minds and hope of all mankind.

Elder Whitney shares the following great insights regarding poets and poetry. I have included this chapter because I feel that the poets we honor and appreciate—Eliza R. Snow, Orson F. Whitney, President Gordon B. Hinckley, Elder Bruce R. McConkie and myriads of others—seem to turn to poetry to honor God and His holy Son. W.W. Phelps and Parley P. Pratt have composed marvelous poetic phrases that have been set to beautiful music and bless us with tender feelings to that Great God of Heaven.

Brother Whitney validates the above with this beautiful sentiment. "They forever reach after and foresee the ultimate good. They are evermore building the paradise that is to be, painting the millennium that is to come, restoring the lost image of God in the human soul." It is my conviction that every word that proceedeth from the mouth of God will be like unto celestial poetry to elevate, comfort, bring peace, vision and understanding to those who look heavenward with love and adoration. This chapter is from poetical writings of Orson F. Whitney, *Juvenile Instructor*, 1889.

"What is the poet good for? and what is the good of poetry? are queries that have doubtless flitted through many a mind, imbued with the idea that nothing is useful which does not in some way increase man's material wealth or minister to his temporal needs...

"This is true of two classes—those who have not poetry, or very little of, in their natures; and those who are brimful of poetry and do not know it; who are really capable of appreciating it, and only need enlightening in order to enjoy to the fullest extent the fragrance and beauty of this flower plucked from the gardens of Paradise and thrown to earth to delight the senses and refresh the souls of lovers of the beautiful and refined....

"Where there is no poetry, there can be little or no eloquence....

"Furthermore, poetry, as expressed in verse, like all other arts and sciences, has its technicalities. The prose reader is puzzled by its transpositions, contractions, ellipses, poetic licenses and rhetorical figures, necessary to rhythm and style, and comparatively unknown in ordinary composition....

"Poetry is that sentiment of the soul, or faculty of the mind, which enables its possessor to appreciate and realize the heights and depths of human experience. It is the power to feel pleasure or suffer pain, in all its exquisiteness and intensity.... Nearly all men and women are poetical, to some extent, but very few can be called poets....The greater the poet, the greater his capacity to suffer and enjoy.... All heights and depths of feeling are theirs;...

"The poetic sentiment or faculty, I have said, is the power to feel intensely, either pleasure or pain. It does not always find expression in words. There are joys that are mute; there are sorrows that never sigh or weep; but are eloquent in their stillness, and all the more powerful for their imprisonment....The most eloquent poets, 'whose words are sparks of immortality,' have felt the painful inadequacy of language to portray their thoughts....

"They who express most, must likewise feel most, of pleasure or pain; and this it is which creates for genius its dual destiny—its laurel wreath of bliss with misery interwoven, its couch of roses with its pillow of thorns. It is one thing to sip the sweets of poesy, and another to provide them for the world's delectation. That which gives us so much pleasure to hear may have caused its author untold toil and pain....

"Says Holland; 'Verily the poets of the world are the prophets of humanity. They forever reach after and foresee the ultimate good. They are evermore building the Paradise that is to be, painting the Millennium that is to come, restoring the lost image of God in the human soul....'

"I am not prepared to admit—nor do I suppose Holland meant to say—that the poets of the world are its only prophets, or that they are prophets in the same sense and degree as the inspired oracles of sacred writ. But I do believe the gift of poesy and the gift of prophecy to be akin to each other; that both are of divine origin, and that they generally go hand in hand. Prophets are almost invariably poets; and poets, in many instances, have been remarkably prophetic. Of the former class attest the writings of David, Isaiah, Jeremiah and others—veritable prophets and veritable poets—who, in some of the grandest poetry ever sung, have indeed 'built the Paradise that is to be, foretold the Millennium that is to come.' Read the parables and sayings of the Savior, you who love poetry and desire to pluck some of its sweetest and most fragrant flowers:

"'Consider the lillies of the field, how they grow; they toil not, neither do they spin, and yet I say unto you that even Solomon, in all his glory, was not arrayed like one of these.'

"Can our language boast anything purer, tenderer, truer and more beautiful? Jesus of Nazareth was a poet, no less than a prophet, of pre-eminent genius.

"Time and your patience would fail me in even glancing over the many conspicuous beauties of Bible poetry....

"Religion is full of poetry, and poetry is full of religion. The loftiest and sublimest, as well as the sweetest and tenderest poetry is religious and cannot be otherwise....

"Poetry is the elder sister of history, the mother of language, the ancestress of civilization....

"His brain has been as the torch of the Almighty to kindle and illumine the nations; his mind the fountain whence have sprung thoughts that have induced millions to think."

Thus it is true, poets and poetry elevate our highest nature toward that great God and His majestic, celestial expressions for the soul of man to feast upon.